THE FIGHTERS OF INDRAPRASTHA

THE SWORDS CLASH

THE FIGHTERS OF INDRAPRASTHA

THE SWORDS CLASH

HIRANMAYI RAM

To my sisters, the queens of their own kingdoms

If you don't fight for what you want, then don't cry for what you lost.

-   Lord Krishna, Bhagavad Gita

CONTENTS

PART ONE

THE SEARCH

THE SWORDS CLASH

SUBHADRAI

IMPENDING DOOM

"Neither in this world or elsewhere is happiness in store for him who always doubts." – Lord Krishna, Bhagavad Gita

You're joking, right?" I asked, desperately turning to the tall, blonde girl next to me, "Please tell me you're joking."

"For the hundredth time," she said, with a groan, "I'm *not*."

I bit my lips, looking straight into her eyes. Was she lying, or was I just super forgetful? It couldn't be the latter.

"Subhadrai," she sighed, standing up from the bench we were sitting on, "Ms. Diana told us a month ago."

"Why would she do that?" I cried, trying to push the blame away, "How are we supposed to remember that? Plus, we *just* had a science test yesterday. Ms. Diana can't be that evil."

Ms. Diana, our math teacher, was *that* evil.

"Come on, Emine," I groaned, "Maybe you got the day wrong. Maybe it's tomorrow."

"It's not,' Emine snapped, picking up her books from the bench, 'And you should hurry up, or we'll be late."

I let out a dramatic groan as I got up and trudged after Emine who kept grumbling about how I never paid attention.

I'm Subhadrai Anand, by the way, and I am NOT forgetful.

At all.

Don't listen to whatever my friend, Emine, tells you. I'm good at remembering *important* things, like when movies come out.

Math tests don't fall under that category… I don't think….

As Emine and I walked down the hallway of Aloe Park Junior High, Emine bumped into Riya M. Ram, another friend of ours who was adopted, like me.

"Guys," she said, bouncing on her toes, "I've been hearing these *really* stupid rumors that there's a math test today. That's totally fake, right?"

I nodded while Emine shook her head.

"Totally fake," I said, putting my hand on Riya's shoulder, "Don't you worry about a thing."

"Hardee harr harr," Emine said, pushing me aside, "We *do* have a test today, Riya."

"Oh," Riya said, frowning, "But Subhadrai just-"

"You can't trust her," Emine pointed out.

"*Hey!*" I protested, turning to Emine, "I'm *very* trustable. You can *see* the trust etched on my face."

Riya pretended to squint at me, then she looked at Emine, "I see what you mean."

"Some friends you are," I grumbled, "You didn't even tell me there was a test!"

"I didn't know about this impending doom!" Riya said, throwing her hands up in the air, smacking a poor passerby in the face.

"How?!" Emine asked, looking at us with shocked expressions, "She told us *last month*."

"That means she told us last year,' Riya pondered, 'Because it's January. Which is quite a big gap."

"Tell me about it," I agreed, as we walked up a metal ramp into our wooden lodge of a classroom.

Normally when we walk into class, we have a picture displayed on the projector and we have to sit down and write a story about the it. Only after we write a one-page story would we start our day.

Instead, there was something else on the projector, and it looked like math.

"One thing I will *never* understand about math is variables," I muttered as we walked in, "Our whole life was spent learning that there was a difference between the alphabet and numbers, and suddenly *x* is a number!"

"I know, right?" Riya said, through the side of her mouth as she sat next to me, 'And don't even get me started on pie.'

We had different seating arrangements for tests and normal class. Emine's test-taking seat was halfway across the room, but Riya and I were right next to each other, which was convenient.

'I'm pretty sure it's pi, spelt without an "e",' I said, furrowing my brows.

'Yeah, whatever, nerd,' Riya muttered as Ms. Diana walked up to the front of the class.

'Okay, everyone, take out your pens, and I'll start handing out the question papers,' Ms. Diana said, clapping.

It was as if fate had turned a switch on causing everyone to groan at the same time, complaining that they didn't know the test existed.

Turns out it was only Emine who remembered so Ms. Diana had no choice but to postpone the test, because there was no point conducting a test in which everyone was going to fail. Plus, I doubt it was an important test.

Once Ms. Diana was done putting the test papers away in her bag, Emine came back to her seat behind me, and Riya went to her seat at the opposite end of the class. That's where Ms. Diana had sent her because she talked far too much.

A few minutes after class started, I glanced at the front of the classroom where Ms. Diana stood with her back to the class. She had absolutely no idea what was going on behind her.

Sofia La Mansion was painting her nails under her desk. Ryan and his friend Devy were at the back of the class making a stock of paper airplanes that could last for a lifetime.

I knew I shouldn't have taken advantage of Ms. Diana's oblivion, but I needed to tell Emine some important news I'd forgotten to tell her in all the math drama. I cautiously turned around and hissed her name.

Emine looked up from her math notebook and realized that the class was in chaos.

"I can't believe I've actually been studying for that test," Emine scowled, slamming her book shut.

Unlike me, Emine didn't care about taking advantage of Ms. Diana's carelessness. Sure, she could be a nerd, but she was a lazy nerd.

She capped her pen and looked at me, "Yeah?"

"Did you hear the song that came out yesterday?" I asked, my eyes shining in excitement.

Yup. That was my important news.

Emine's face brightened, and her voice went up an octave, 'Oh my god! YES! It was amazing! I love that part at the-'

"Emine," Ms. Diana snapped from the front of the class, "Please turn your volume down."

Emine and I looked at Ms. Diana to check if she'd turned around, but that was too much to expect from her. Her eyes stayed fixed upon the board, her hand moving swiftly across it.

After a few minutes, once Sofia had finished painting the nails on her right hand, Ms. Diana turned around. I love it when she turns around because the expression on everyone's face is *delightful.* I don't mean to say that I love it when people panic, but... I love it when people panic.

I looked around the room, enjoying the shifting atmosphere. Sofia's nail polish bottle had disappeared, and her left hand lay across her right hand covering the bright pink paint.

Devy and Ryan, the two boys at the back of the class, had sat up straight, their pens in their hands writing down everything Ms. Diana had written on the board with smiles etched on their faces. The stack of airplanes was pushed onto the floor behind their fat bags.

Ms. Diana smiled at the class proudly, "Alright class, that's it. You guys can wrap up for today. Pack up your bags."

Emine smirked as Ms. Diana left the room, "I wonder what would happen if she ever watched the video footage."

I stared at the CCTV at the corner of the room, frowning, "I doubt it works."

Emine laughed, "Yeah, this school's too broke to buy anything past a No. 2 Pencil. I still want to know, though."

The two of us walked out of the class, our bags slung over our shoulders, chortling. As we walked past the row of lockers gossiping about the latest books and whatnot, I bumped into one of Sofia's friends, Luxury.

"Watch it, nerd," she snapped as she walked past me.

Emine snorted and I glared at her.

For some reason everyone in the school thought I was a nerd (A fact that made everyone who really knew me fall on the floor laughing).

Emine rolled her eyes, "Imagine if everyone in the school found out that your last math mark was a-"

"We don't talk about that," I said quickly, cutting her off.

Emine grinned, "Yeah, nobody cares anyways."

Emine had complete potential to be popular, but she told me that anyone who *was* popular was a jerk who didn't know how to read good books. I didn't argue.

At the end of the day, as I was packing my bag, Ms. Diana called me, "Subhadrai, I told you to remind the class a week before the test, remember?"

I scrunched my forehead trying to recall, "Not really."

"Subhadrai, I made you the class monitor with a sense of trust," Ms. Diana sighed, "I thought you would keep that trust, but you've proved me wrong. I suppose you're not cut out to be a leader after all."

I watched her as she walked away down the metal ramp, a boiling sensation in my stomach. Boy, teachers are the *best* at making you feel like you're the worst person in the world.

A leader…

I felt my eyes burn, and I wiped my eyes quickly, hoping nobody would notice. I spotted Emine turning away from the corner of my eye, and I felt like I was about to go all out. I quickly walked towards the bathroom stalls and as I stood there, leaning against the door, staring at the ceiling, Ms. Diana's words replayed in my head.

I suppose you're not cut out to be a leader after all.

I blinked rapidly trying to pull myself together. I suppose not…

****

Emine and I were waiting in line for the bus when my backpack was rammed.

"Agh!" I yelled as my folder went flying to the ground.

I regained my balance in time to see Rohan Sharma shove by.

"I can't believe you used to be friends with that jerk," Emine said, picking up my papers.

I rubbed my now sore shoulder tenderly, "That was two years ago. He doesn't even talk to me now. Not even long enough to say sorry for nearly knocking me over, apparently."

"Did you drop this?" my sister, Amrita said, walking up to me, "Stop being so clumsy, Subhadrai."

She chortled and walked into the bus past me.

I rolled my eyes. Little sisters were such brats.

Emine pointed to a seat at the back of the bus, "Let's go sit there."

I nodded and walked over to the chair. Emine rushed in before me and I was stuck in the aisle, which I really didn't like. I don't get why Amrita and I even took the bus, though. Our school, Aloe Park, was so close to our house, we could walk, and we'd reach our home at the same time as the bus. I guess our mother wanted us to fit in with the other kids. Not that it was working....

As the bus screeched to a halt at the end of our street, Arionto Common, Amrita and I trudged out of the bus. At once, she turned to me.

"So," she smirked, "Did you have that math test?"

"How did you know about that?" I asked, squinting my eyes.

"You told me to remind you a month ago."

"Well, why didn't you?" I asked furiously.

She opened the door, ignoring me, and walked in leaving me to fume. As I dropped my bag at the foot of the stairs, I heard Amma talking on the phone (Amma was what I called my mother).

"She's only twelve, we can't send them already. Don't tell me about Satya. She was raised there," Amma was saying, "Has Sahana arrived?"

A muffled voice at the other end said something.

Amma turned to look at the doorway of the kitchen and saw me standing there with a puzzled look on my face. Who was she talking about?

Our eyes met for a second and she quickly pulled away.

"Look, she's not interested in gymnastics classes, okay?" Amma said, hesitantly.

She hung up on the person at the other end and looked up at me with a smile, "You're home early."

"No," I insisted, "It's two forty-five."

Amma checked the clock, "Oh. Well then, I should probably start making lunch."

I sat down at the dining table opposite to the kitchen and said, "I wouldn't mind gymnastics classes."

Amma looked at me, confused, "What? Oh *those*. You have no time."

I shrugged, not bothering to argue. My father, Vidura (I call him Appa), walked down the stairs smiling.

"Who wants to watch a movie?" he asked, holding the TV remote up.

Amrita ran down from her room and ended up bumping into our dad.

"YESSSS!" She screamed, running into the living room, plopping herself onto a couch with a huge sigh.

Appa smiled and winked at Amma, "Alright, Subhadrai, what would *you* like to watch?"

I shrugged, frowning, "Beats me."

If I did choose, I'd end up choosing something no one else liked.

Again, I heard Ms. Diana's voice, *I suppose you're not cut out to be a leader after all.*

Amrita raised her hand, "Oooh! Oooh! I have an idea!!!'

So, we spent the next two hours watching a bunch of guys beat up other guys. Yay.

***

The next day at school, during Ms. Diana's class, Emine tapped my back and asked, "Have you ever been to India?"

I snorted, "Uh, duh. I literally went two months ago to visit my grandparents."

"Where do you normally stay?" she asked.

I crinkled my brows, "Why are you asking me this?"

Emine ignored me, turning serious, "You didn't tell me that you and Rohan are family friends!"

I looked at her, baffled, "What?"

She knew full well that Rohan had stopped talking to me two years ago when he moved here. Why would she think we were friends?

"You always acted so rude to him, and he acted rude to you," Emine said, "I thought you hated each other. You could've *told* me you guys were super close! Close enough to go to India together!"

I laughed, "I would need to know that to tell you."

Emine stared at me, "You *do* know who I'm talking about, don't you? The one on the school basketball team who lives in a mansion?"

An image of Rohan shoving past me on the bus came to my mind, "We're definitely not friends."

Emine frowned, "But Mr. D said you were."

Mr. D was our science teacher. He was not the sort of guy I'd be talking to about my relationship with Rohan.

I choked, "Excuse me?"

"Uh, yeah," Emine murmured, "He told me that I should keep your tests when he hands them out later, because your parents told him that you and Rohan would be in India. You *really* don't know about this?"

I nodded, rolling my eyes, "Pretty sure."

That afternoon, during lunch Amrita walked up to me, "Hey Subhadrai. Are we going to India?"

I choked.

"WHY IS EVERYONE ASKING ME THIS?!" I whisper-screamed, making some people stare, "I DON'T KNOW, OKAY?"

I get stressed out when I don't know the answer to something. I was unreliable enough, but if I'd forgotten something as major as an India trip, I'd *never* hear the end of it.

I felt a pang in my chest, and I tried to ignore the feeling.

I suppose you're not cut out to be a leader after all.

Why did I care? I was never going to be a leader anyways.

"Sheesh, I was only asking," Amrita said, haughtily, "Calm down."

I rolled my eyes and sat down at the seventh graders' table with Emine.

"Why does everyone think I'm going to India," I grumbled, taking my lunch out of my bag.

As if Emine and Amrita were everyone.

Emine giggled, "I asked Rohan. He totally ignored me."

"Oh really?" I asked, sighing, "What else is new?"

Emine opened her lunch box, "Definitely not my lunch. These are last night's leftovers."

I peeked into her box and retched, "Yeah, I *really* needed that today, didn't I?"

After lunch, as I was walking to class, Rohan stopped me.

"Listen," he said, darkly, "Stop spreading rumors. I hardly know you. Why would I go to India with you?"

He hardly knew me? The only person in the school who knew me more than Amrita was him.

I threw my hands up, frustrated, "*I'm* spreading rumors? *Excuse* me! I'm pretty sure you've been telling everyone that *I'm* going to India! Seriously, it's not funny. Stop it."

Rohan stared at me for a second, his black beady eyes eying mine, "Just... forget we talked about this, okay?"

I rolled my eyes, "Like I would want to remember it."

I shouldn't have said that, because that was all I thought about for the rest of the day. If *Rohan* didn't know and Amrita and *I* didn't know, but my science teacher Mr. D knew, then something was really wrong.

13

SUBHADRAI

MY CAR HAS A SPEAR IN IT?!

"What belongs to you belonged to someone yesterday, and will be someone else's tomorrow" – Lord Krishna, Bhagavad Gita

Amrita followed me into the house the next afternoon to see Amma frantically running around the house.

"VIDURA!" Amma screamed, "Where are the car keys?!"

"In the basement," Appa called, from the basement.

"Well then, give it!" Amma hollered, looking down the staircase to see my dad walking up with a sigh.

Amma grabbed it from him and yanked her coat off its stand.

"Where are you going?" Amrita asked, dumping her bag into a pile of other random assortments.

"*We* are going somewhere important," Amma said, turning to Amrita and me, "Get dressed into a *kurti* and get in the car."

Once we'd walked down, wearing our ancient *kurtis*, Amma was standing at the doorway looking impatient, "Quick, girls."

Amrita and I looked at each other, confused, but followed Amma into the car.

"We were supposed to do this *yesterday*," Amma muttered to herself, shaking her head.

"Is this a dentist appointment?" Amrita asked as the car left the driveway, "In that case, no matter how many cavities I have, I'm not-"

"It's not a dentist appointment," Amma said, "But that does remind me…."

The car sped down the streets of Fremont, California as Amma started talking.

"The Mahabharata," she said, sounding slightly panicked, "Is a story about a war for the throne."

I frowned, "Huh?"

That was random.

"It started with two brothers," she continued, eyeing me through the rearview mirror, "Their names were Dhritarastra and Pandu."

I turned to look at Amrita in confusion, "What is she saying?"

"Subhadrai, listen," Amma said, impatiently, "We don't have much time."

"What is *that* supposed to mean?" Amrita asked.

Amma's phone started ringing, and she declined it.

"Dhritarashtra was the eldest," Amma said, placing her phone on the seat next to her, "But he wasn't allowed to rule, because he was born blind."

"That's not fair," I said, "I think-"

"Listen! Pandu became king, but he was eventually exiled, and Dhritarastra became king after all," Amma swerved sharply past a corner, and stopped her phone from falling, "Pandu had five children, the Pandavas."

"Why are you *saying* this?" Amrita said, "Can we listen to music instead."

"Amrita, keep your mouth *shut*," Amma said, anger creeping into her voice, "The sons of Pandu were named Yudhisthira, Bhima, Arjuna, Nakula and Sahadeva."

"Those are complicated names," I laughed, "Do we need to remember them?"

"Yes! Stop interrupting me!" Amma said, and her phone started ringing again.

She ignored it and kept talking over the music, "Dhritarastra had a hundred kids, the oldest of which was Duryodhana and his younger brother Dussasana."

"A hundred!" Amrita gasped.

"The Pandavas wanted the kingdom because it was *their* father who was ruling it first, and out of the hundred and five kids, Yudhishthira was the eldest, and hence, the rightful heir," She said, "But *Dhritarastra's* kids, called the Kauravas, believed that Duryodhana, the direct firstborn of the *current* king should rule."

She turned into a smaller street and drove past a golden gate.

"The Pandavas and Kauravas had a war to decide the next ruler," Amma said, "And in the end-"

There was a thud as something hit the car, and Amma stopped in a start. I fell forward and hit myself on the seat in front of me.

As I was rubbing my chin, Amma's phone started ringing again, and she picked it up with a sigh, "Myna, I'm here. Calm down!"

There was a pause.

"What? My car has a spear in it?"

Amma stepped outside and her eyes widened. That's when a lady came running towards Amma and whispered something to her, laughing.

My eyes met the lady's and she smiled.

Amma gestured for us to get out of the car, and as I stepped outside and looked, my eyes widened.

There were kids running around brandishing swords, bows, and shields. I whirled around looking at Amma who didn't look surprised.

Follow me, she mouthed, and walked into a building with the other lady.

Hotel K, USA, read a sign in front of the building in dark purple.

We came to a halt in front of a door labeled *Office*.

Outside the room was…

"Shyamala!" I said, breaking into a grin.

The girl looked at me, "Hey Subhadrai. You too?"

"What?" I looked at her quizzically.

Shyamala was my dad's sister's adopted daughter. She lived in North Carolina, so I had *no* idea what she was doing here.

"Subhadrai," Amma hissed, "Come in."

Amrita and I walked into the office where the lady was sitting at a desk, shuffling through a pile of papers.

"Yo, Diya, sit," the lady said, gesturing to three chairs in front of her desk.

"This is what Amma was so tense for," Amrita whispered to me with a smirk.

I snorted.

"Well," the lady said, fixing her gaze on Amrita and me, 'If it isn't Subhadrai and Amrita!'

We stared at her in confusion.

"I'm Myna," she said, grinning, "Daughter of Savitri, head of KOMC."

We blinked, "Eh?"

"Savitri," Myna prompted, "From the story... Never mind. You wouldn't know."

"What's KOMC?" Amrita asked.

Amma looked at Myna expectantly.

"Alright," Myna said, leaning back, "I guess we should get started. KOMC stands for Kids of Mythological Characters. Mythological characters include people like my parents, or it could include-"

"The Pandavas," Amrita finished, "So, *that's* what that story was about."

"Exactly," the lady nodded, "So, the Pandavas are-"

"Ancient mythological characters from the Mahabharata," I said, wisely "We know."

Myna smirked, "I was about to say, 'your parents'."

"What?" I said, sure I'd heard her wrong.

"The Pandavas," Myna said, slowly, "are your parents. Well, technically, not *all* of them. Subhadrai, *you* are the daughter of Bhima. Amrita, you're the daughter of Nakula. Your cousin, Shyamala, is the daughter of Sahadeva."

Amrita and I shot each other a skeptical look.

"Okay, jokes aside," I said, "Why are we here?"

Amma and Myna blinked at me, "What joke?"

"Obviously this is some sort of practical joke," I said, slowly, "Are you our therapist or something?"

"Or a dentist," Amrita said, filled with suspicion.

Myna let out a loud laugh, "I'm not joking!"

Amma let out a faint hint of a smile, "We're telling the truth."

There was a knock on the door and two other girls walked in with Shyamala.

"Subhadrai and Amrita," Myna said, "Meet your siblings."

SUBHADRAI

WHAT WAS I GETTING MYSELF INTO?

"To whom pleasure, and pain are the same, is fit for attaining immortality." – Lord Krishna, Bhagavad Gita

I had to admit the whole thing hardly seemed believable at first. That was until Myna showed the other girls, Amrita and I hardcore proof.

"Look," she said, "I know that all four of you are having trouble believing the whole circumstance, so I pulled some strings and brought a god to America."

She stepped aside to reveal a man standing in the hallway glowering at us.

"Is this them?" he asked, squinting at us.

Myna nodded.

"Well?" said one of the new girls with long undone hair and a faint British accent.

The man raised his eyebrows and burst into flames.

I felt my jaw drop, "Oh gods…"

"I," said the man, "am Agni, the god of fire. I hope you're pleased."

He waited for applause but didn't get it.

The girl with the British accent frowned, "There are plenty of scientific ways in which that could happen."

Agni groaned, "Of *course* there is. No! I am a real deva (an Indian god), thank you very much! Tell me, daughter of Arjuna, is there a scientific explanation for this?"

Agni rose off the ground and hovered over Myna's desk, the jewels on his cylindrical golden crown glinting. With a flick of his hand, the table combusted. Once the flames flickered away, the desk sat there, perfectly intact, without the slightest hint of a scar, but there *was* a coffee stain I doubt Agni had created.

The girl (who was apparently the daughter of Arjuna the third Pandava) fell silent.

Agni haughtily sniffed and disappeared in a flash of light.

My mind reeled trying to process what was going on. My thoughts felt like a stack of paper in front of a table fan.

Should I trust Myna?

Should I run away screaming for the police?

The second option sure would be cooler, but I didn't feel like it. Partially because I was too lazy to run and partially because I *did* trust Myna.

"Well, Sahana?" Myna said to the daughter of Arjuna, "Are you satisfied?"

Sahana nodded, still looking surprised and confused.

"I hope all of you are," Myna smiled, "Tomorrow, you start training. Ya'll should be here by four in the afternoon, alright?"

***

"Hey," Riya said, looking up from her book as I walked into class, "You ready for that test?"

"You think too high of me," I rolled my eyes.

It'd been late when we got home from Hotel K last night, and Amma hadn't let me stay up to study.

"Emine is going to *kill* you," Riya snorted.

Sofia La Mansion, the nail polish girl, walked over to Riya and smacked a piece of paper in front of her, "What is *this* supposed to be?"

Riya glanced at the paper, and shrugged, "How am I supposed to know."

"It's a letter to Ms. Diana," Sofia snarled, "Can you guess what it says?"

Riya picked the paper up and skimmed through it, "It's a complaint. Says you aren't paying attention during class."

Sofia pulled out another sheet which had a picture of her applying nail polish on her hand during math yesterday.

"Woah," Riya said, "You're in big trouble."

"Oh, really? I hadn't noticed," Sofia said, "You know whose fault it is? Yours. You sent this, *didn't* you?"

Riya glanced at me, perplexed, "No…"

"Don't lie, loser," Sofia sniffed, "You know what I'm going to do? My dad is going to-"

"Shut up, Sofia," I snapped, "She didn't do it."

"Oh, so *you* did, Anand?" Sofia said, turning to me menacingly.

I tried to find the words to tell her I hadn't, but I froze. Why did I speak up? Sofia's glare seemed to last forever.

I felt a shiver run down my spine as she crumpled up the paper and balled her fists.

"No," I muttered, shuffling my feet.

Why was I like this? I was a daughter of Bhima! The strongest Pandava there was!

"Hey, Sofia," called a voice from the doorway, "Did you and Ms. Diana have your chat yesterday?"

Sofia whirled around in fury as Emine walked over, "You!"

"Are you surprised? Why? Nobody else is surprised," Emine said, looking at me with a wink.

I didn't say anything. My voice had died with my confidence.

"Yeah, Sofia," Riya said, playing along, "How could you *not* know that? What were you saying? Your dad was going to…?"

Sofia glared at Emine whose dad was Sofia's dad's boss. She stuck her tongue out at Emine like a three-year-old and stormed away.

"So," Emine said, walking over to me, "Did you study?"

"Oh yeah," I lied, with a smirk, "*So* hard. That's all I did last night."

That's when Devy ran in with a grin, "Ms. Diana's absent!!"

I turned to Emine who looked like she could kill him, "Too bad! I was *really* looking forward to that math test."

****

I ran down the stairs, quickly tying my hair in a braid as Amrita rushed into the car. Amma had given us these really comfy purple shirts which were apparently part of the uniform for the hotel.

My school didn't have a uniform, so I was thrilled to finally blend in with everyone.

"Get in!" Amma screamed from the car.

I stopped admiring my shirt and swung the door open, smacking myself in the face. Amrita was sitting in the passenger seat, tapping her feet excitedly.

"What will they train us to do?" she asked.

"I'm not sure," Amma said, sounding worried, "Don't kill anyone, okay?"

I laughed, nervously, "That was a joke, right?"

She pursed her lips and shrugged.

What was I getting myself into?!

****

"Here," Myna said, handing me a sword, "You hold it like this."

I gasped as I felt the cold metal of the sword in my palm. I traced my finger across the engraving of the lion in awe.

Was this even allowed? Could a twelve-year-old wield a sword? Most importantly, could I use it at school?

I grinned thinking about how I'd walk up into school with my sword, decked in armor, and brandish it in front of Sofia.

That'd teach her that I don't need a ponytail so high my nose bled to be popular.

"Space out your hands like this," Myna said, shattering my thoughts.

The British girl, Sahana dropped her sword with a frightened yelp.

"Are you sure we won't die?" Shyamala asked, holding her sword as far away from herself as possible.

Myna nodded, "Don't worry. Plus, you and Amrita are the *grandchildren* of the gods of healing. I'm sure you can help us if anything happens."

They were? I thought Pandu was our grandfather. I told Myna that.

"He is," Myna nodded, "But each of you were born with the blessing of a god. Like you, Subhadrai, are the grandchild of Vayu, God of wind."

"Me?" Sahana asked, excitedly.

"You're the child of Indra, king of the gods," Myna smiled, proudly, "Now, pay attention."

"Why are we even learning this?" Amrita asked.

The tall girl next to Sahana answered this time, "Because we might have to fight in war eventually. I'm Satya, the daughter of Yudhishthira, by the way."

"War?" I asked, my heart racing, "What? Why?"

"Later," Myna said, "First, learn."

She demonstrated holding the sword and slashed the air a few times.

I gripped my lion sword and drew in a deep breath as Myna taught us how to attack.

Who were we fighting against?

I brought my sword forward to Amrita and stepped towards her.

"No, no," Myna shook her head, "You have a *sword* in your hand! If you want to live, you can't step towards your opponent like that!"

She pushed me aside and demonstrated.

Amrita seemed to pick it up quickly and Myna started teaching her how to use a mace.

Meanwhile Satya was teaching Sahana how to string a bow. I stood in the corner of the field looking at Shyamala and Amrita fence.

"Don't worry, Subhadrai," Myna said, walking up to me after making sure Amrita and Shyamala wouldn't kill each other, "You're the daughter of Bhima. Whatever weapon you choose, you'll pick it up eventually."

I nodded uncertainly, but didn't say anything.

"Here," Myna said, realizing that I hadn't cheered up, "Let me show you something."

She held my hand, and there was a bright flash of light and I felt like a thousand rocks were falling on my head. When the light dimmed out, we were on the other side of the field.

I retched, doubling over, and I could feel Myna's trust in me ever learning how to do anything crash into the pits of hell.

"I did that too," came the daughter of Yudhishthira's voice from behind me.

She handed me a glass of water and I drank.

"It's good that you don't like it," Satya said, "If you do it too many times, light-travelling can be dangerous."

I smiled in appreciation as Myna walked away to help Amrita whose mace had gotten stuck in Sahana's bow.

"Come on, let's try again," Satya said, holding my hand.

SUBHADRAI

WE'RE GOING FIRST CLASS.

'Knowing is not enough, we must apply. Willing is not enough, we must do.' - Lord Krishna, Bhagavad Gita

L isten," Emine said, examining the math test I'd written last week, "You need to work on your decimal division. Look, you made a mistake here-"

"Yeah, Emine," I sighed, "I know."

It'd been a month since we'd started training, and last night I'd slept over at the hotel and Satya had driven me to school, which is why Amrita, and I were wearing our crumpled purple t-shirts.

"You haven't been in a good mood, lately," Emine glanced at Riya who shrugged.

I knew I probably *was* being annoying, but wasn't that my job as a best friend? I hadn't really clarified with Myna how secretive I was supposed to be about the KOMC thing either, but I was pretty sure that even if I told Emine I was training to become a warrior she wouldn't believe me.

It's not my fault I wasn't focusing on math or whatever it was we were doing. My mind was so wrapped up in training, I couldn't focus on anything! Amrita was getting straight B's, and I was getting straight C's. Not the best records, if you ask me.

I sighed and got up, "Okay, let's go."

"Where?" Emine asked, getting up too.

"Class," I said, plodding towards the exit of the cafeteria.

"We still have twenty minutes for lunch to end," Emine said, clutching at straws, "We could go to the basketball court! We'll work on your dribble-"

"I think I'll go to class," I said, absentmindedly bumping into someone.

"Watch it, Anand," Rohan snapped.

I'd forgotten all about him, and the sight of him made my stomach drop.

"What *happened* between you two?" Riya asked, rolling her eyes at him.

I sighed dramatically "I *would* tell the two of you, except you wouldn't believe me if I did!"

I was lying. I had no idea why he was angry at me or why I was getting monthly glares and shoves from him.

I figured Emine would make out my bluff, but she didn't.

"Wow!" she said, rolling her eyes, "I *would*, Subhadrai. Why can't you try? You have to get people to trust you if you ever want to *do* anything."

I stopped, "*Excuse* me? Well, at least *I* can deal with being alone! You can't even do that!"

I immediately regretted saying that. I opened my mouth to apologize, but Emine cut me off.

"Well, I'll never have to be alone, because I'm nothing like you," Emine said, making some people stare, "And I-"

"Woah, woah, woah," Riya said, signaling for us to calm down, "Chill. This is *not* the time."

"I can argue whenever I like, Riya," I said, nastily, "Especially when a certain someone is being a jerk."

"I think someone wants to talk to you, Subhadrai," Riya said, slowly.

I followed her gaze and spotted the new member in our little conversation, "What the-"

I had never expected to see her at my school, and I wasn't *prepared* to see her until this afternoon.

"I'm sorry, Emine," said Satya as I stared in shock, "I'm Subhadrai's cousin. I'm going to need her for a little bit, okay? Thanks!"

She pulled me to the side and gave me a packet of *Mentos*, "Here."

I took it, "What are you *doing* here?!"

"Bhisma's calling you guys in early. It's my job to get you. We need to go to the Sharma house."

Bhishma? Who was that?

In? In where?

And the Sharma house? What was *that?*

"Who's Bhishma?" I asked.

"He's your great granduncle, and the supreme commander of the Kaurava army," Satya said, checking the time on her phone, "Follow me?"

"What does 'supreme commander' mean?" I wondered aloud.

"He's the eldest in our family. He makes the big decisions, and has control over what happens," Satya explained.

"Oh," I said.

Despite all the training, I still didn't feel like a *Pandava* yet, and all the family information felt good. Like I was finally a part of something.

"Where does he want us to go?" I asked, as Satya stopped outside of Amrita's classroom.

"India," Satya said.

I looked at her for a beat, "Why?"

"Rohan's started recruiting armies for war," Satya said.

"Rohan?" I asked.

"The son of Duryodhana," Satya explained.

Amrita came out of the room with her bag over her shoulder.

"Come on," Satya grabbed our shoulders and we light-traveled away.

I'd gotten a whole lot better at the whole light-travel thing, and this time, when we landed in front of my house, I didn't throw up.

"Alright, *now* can you tell me what we're doing here?" Amrita asked, impatiently.

"I thought we were going to the Sharma house?" I asked.

"We were, but I don't want to," Satya said, as if she were deciding it then.

Amma came out of the house when a taxi pulled up.

"Get in," Satya told me, and went over to the driver and told him to go to the airport.

Amrita, Amma and I got into the car as Satya disappeared to collect Sahana and Shyamala.

"Who's Rohan?" I asked Amma.

She looked at me, "Huh?"

"The son of Duryodhana? I feel like I should know," I said, "And why do we have to go to India if he starts recruiting armies."

Amma bit her lip as if she knew, but didn't want to say, "I suppose it means you're on the brink of war."

****

I walked down the aisle of the airplane and sat next to Sahana.

"Hi," I sat down.

"Hello," she said, smiling.

"So," I asked, tapping my fingers together, "How's life?"

Despite being together for a month, we hadn't spoken much, making the whole situation awkward.

"Good," she said, fastening her seatbelt, "You?"

"Good," I snapped my belt together too.

I could feel her gaze on me, waiting for me to talk. I racked my brain trying to think of something interesting to say.

Sahana eventually processed that I had nothing to say when I let out a 'So…?'

"It's hard to digest, isn't it? All this happened so quickly! I bet it's normal for Satya, though. She's been trained her whole life," she said, energetically, "Because she was the most likely candidate for the throne."

"The throne," I repeated through gritted teeth, gripping the handles of the chair as the plane took off.

"Yeah," Sahana said as the flight attendant gestured for her to lean back, "Nobody told us anything about what's going on, so I called Satya last night for a tell-all interview."

"What did she tell you?" I asked curiously.

"Apparently the gods (the *Devas*) have no longer been respected as much as they felt that they should've been. That angered them a lot. So, then they went and complained to Brahma (who'd *never* been respected by humans because of a curse he'd received) who knew how they felt. Brahma was known as the "creator" because according to legend he created life on Earth."

"Lemme guess," I said, "Brahma decided to create the Mahabharata again, because during the Mahabharata they were respected?"

Sahana nodded, "Brahma also used some sort of magic to convince everyone that India's been under monarchy the whole time. All the famous mythological characters were reborn. Although one thing did go amiss in Brahma's plan. He assumed that the Pandavas and Kauravas would immediately hate each other."

"They didn't?" I asked.

The way Amma had said it made it seem like the Pandavas and Kauravas hated each other hard.

"Yeah. As they grew, the Pandavas and Kauravas regained their memories from their previous births, so they were kind to one another. Everything seemed to be fine for a while. That *was* until Rohan was born. Then, even though it was already decided that Satya would rule, Duryodhana secretly trained Rohan for ten years instead of sending him away like us."

The plane shook, and Sahana looked up.

We watched Satya walk over to where Myna was.

"You didn't finish!" I complained mostly to myself.

Unfinished stories tended to kill me on the inside. I recalled Amma not finishing the story of the Mahabharata and felt nauseous.

"Oh, sorry," Sahana laughed, "What do *you* think happens?"

"I don't know. The Pandavas found out that Rohan has been training for kingship then they try to kill him or something. Then they started arguing and then started a war. That's why we're being called back. To fight," I shrugged.

I recalled Amma saying we were on the brink of war. It seemed far more believable now.

"That seemed oddly specific," Sahana frowned.

"I read a lot," I looked at Satya who was talking to Myna rapidly.

Satya turned and gestured for Sahana and I to follow her.

The two of us got up and joined Amrita, Shyamala, Myna, and Satya.

"We need to get off the plane," Myna whispered, "My brother, Vijay, has reported that a Kaurava is on board."

Sahana and I glanced at each other nervously, our footsteps echoing across the cabin.

"We're going first class," Myna said, pointing to a cream curtain.

"Shocking. So am I," said a voice behind us.

We spun around to see...

"Rohan?" I was shocked.

"You know him?" Sahana asked me as Myna drew a dagger.

"Stay away, Rohan," Myna scowled, "Don't do anything. They haven't hurt anyone."

"Shut up, Myna," Rohan snapped, "I'm not here for you."

His eyes moved to me, and he drew a dagger of his own, "I'm here for our queen."

I couldn't move. Rohan? Rohan Sharma?

Why did I not put two and two together? The *Sharma* house!

And Satya was talking about a Rohan too... what was she saying?

As Myna pushed me behind her, it clicked. He was the son of Duryodhana.

Is *that* why he started ignoring me? He was trained until he was ten when the Pandavas and Kauravas started fighting! That was two years ago! The revelation made me gasp.

Then I decided that if I ever told Emine this, she would *never* believe me.

Rohan didn't even bat a lash when he pushed past Satya towards me.

I processed what he had said. Our queen….

Who was that?

Satya patted her pockets growing panicked.

"You can't kill Subhadrai," Myna said, stepping in front of me blocking Rohan's path, "If you lay one finger on her…"

Me? Why would Rohan want to kill me?

"You'll make your *army* track me down," Rohan sighed, sounding slightly amused, "I'm sorry, Myna. You may be older than me, but you're pretty stupid for twenty-six."

He tried to plunge the dagger into Myna's gut, but she deflected it with her own dagger.

"What has your father done?" Myna asked, looking at Rohan, full of regret, as she deflected more of his attempts to get past her.

Rohan went towards Myna full of fury when she mentioned his father, but Myna sidestepped, making him crash into a shelf of supplies. Myna shook her head.

"They never learn," she said, grabbing my wrist.

She pulled me away from the cabin with the other four following uncertainly, but all I could think about was Rohan calling me the queen.

I suppose you're not cut out to be a leader after all.

Myna pulled out her phone and dialed a number as Satya took out a dagger from her bag. All the other passengers were staring, so she smiled and told someone she was an actress for an action movie, and they were about to film.

Rohan walked in glaring at us when Myna ended the call.

'Run,' Myna whispered, "Go to the back. I'll follow you."

I started running with the eyes of every passenger on me. When I reached the back, I found someone waiting.

"Who are you?" He asked, slowly.

"Daughter of Bhima," I said in a rush.

If it was someone who would help us, he would understand. If he was a normal human being, he would think I'd gone mad. If he was an enemy, I would be dead.

"Ah," said the man, "You're Subhadrai, aren't you?"

The rest of the group entered the compartment I was in, earning dirty glares from the passengers. Myna followed, looking out of breath, but pleased.

"Alright, then," said the man, "Follow me."

He walked down the aisle and stopped in front of an open emergency exit. That's when Rohan entered with a large maroon gash running down the side of his face.

The man smiled, "So *this* is the Kaurava spawn you all are so worried about? What a lump of meat."

Rohan growled, staring at the open emergency exit, "*Excuse* me. And who are *you* supposed to be?"

A lot of the passengers had started staring in awe as if this *was* a movie scene after all, but the flight attendant wasn't buying it. She kept trying to speak but was afraid she might ruin a perfect sequence. No one questioned the fact that there wasn't a camera.

"Vayu," the man said, clicking the hatch open, "God of wind."

I gasped. Hadn't Myna mentioned that Vayu was my grandfather? I could feel a scream of excitement building in my throat.

He jumped out and floated in the air making everyone stare. The passengers were probably impressed. This "movie" was going to rock!

"Well," he beckoned, "Come on."

Myna didn't hesitate and followed. She (fortunately) didn't go plummeting and floated along with the god.

That was a good sign.

The passengers were starting to grow suspicious. Satya and Shyamala tentatively stepped into the air and floated. Sahana and I glanced at each other.

She shrugged and followed Satya and Shyamala. Amrita and I sighed.

"I cannot believe this is happening," I muttered.

"Don't worry," Vayu said, "Their memories will be erased by the end of the flight along with any footage of us."

I wasn't worrying about that. I was worrying more about jumping off the plane.

It was around this time that Rohan got over his shock of meeting a god and started advancing.

"Come on, Subhadrai," He said, "I *need* you right now. I'm your friend, remember? The Kauravas don't *have* to be bad."

I turned to look at him, blood dripping off his face.

"Um," I looked at Myna who was furiously gesturing for me to step out of the plane.

Rohan took another two steps towards me, and Amrita scurried into the air. I glanced at her and then Rohan.

"Well," Rohan said, "Do you choose *me*, your childhood friend, or these strangers with crazy stories."

I frowned, glancing behind me at Vayu who was muttering impatiently, "Why do *I* get the coward?"

"SUBHADRAI, FOR ONCE YOU NEED TO LET GO OF WHATEVER HAPPENED IN THE PAST," Amrita hollered impatiently, "JUST GET OFF THE PLANE."

I tried to remember him pushing past me on the bus. Yet, all I could see was his face, right now as he held out his hand for me.

I stepped back, onto the comfort of the wind as the breeze rushed onto my face and we glided away from Rohan's furious screams.

***

Myna decided that it was best if the children of the Pandavas (a.k.a. us) don't stay with the rest of the KOMC. She thought that the Kauravas might have spies there and they would try to stop us from reaching our full potential (whatever that meant). She took us to an empty field on the outskirts of Hastinapura where she opened up a drain (I was sure that she had gone mad. Maybe I should've gone with Rohan).

Apparently, it was a cleverly disguised opening to an... underground palace. I would never have guessed that.

She told us we'd be staying here for the night, and she'd update us on what was going to happen next, but who could sleep after all this?

SUBHADRAI

OUT OF THE LOOP

"Change is the law of nature" – Lord Krishna, Bhagavad Gita

That night, I fell asleep a lot quicker than I imagined, but it wasn't for long. I pulled myself out the bed at around three in the morning.

I walked over to the hall where I heard someone talking in hushed tones. Pressing my ear to the wooden door, I could barely make out what the person was saying.

"I can't come right now," came Myna's voice, "Is Rohan still there?"

I frowned. Where?

"No? How could you let him light-travel away?!" Myna's volume increased a bit, "Has everyone left the building?"

There was a scream at the other end, and Myna sighed.

"Fine, I'll try to come."

There was the sound of the phone being placed on a table and a flash of light. I waited for a minute and slowly creaked the door open.

"Myna?" I whispered.

She wasn't there.

I was about to leave when I heard the soft *ping* of a text message. I went over to the source of the sound and picked the phone up.

It was a message from a lady named Draupadi.

Bring the girls here tomorrow, it read.

I couldn't *not* be curious. The girls? That had to be us.

I clicked a button on the side and the phone logged in automatically. I zoomed in on the picture of the lady who'd sent the message.

As the picture appeared, I gasped.

It was like staring at a mirror. I squinted at the picture. It was a lady who looked a bit older than me. Her dark brown eyes were like diamonds on her bronze skin.

I gazed at the image. I knew that I'd seen that face before.

It was as if *my* face had been photoshopped into *her* face.

I felt my heartbeat quicken. If Bhima was my father, then...

I went to the web and searched up who the wife of Bhima was.

"Draupadi," I gasped.

***

I was already awake when Satya, Sahana, Amrita and Shyamala came out. I'd gone to bed after I'd seen the picture, but I hadn't slept.

Myna had come back at around three in the morning, taken her phone, and left.

She hadn't noticed I was awake, which I was grateful for. If she *had*, she probably would've asked me why I was awake.

What would I have said? *I've just seen my* mother. *Of course I'm awake.* Well technically, she wasn't *my* mother.

Draupadi had married all *five* of the Pandavas.

"You're up early," Amrita noticed, then turned to Shyamala, "Remember that Sunday when she woke up at one p.m.?"

Shyamala giggled, "Oh, yeah."

Sahana smiled at me, "I've woken up later."

"Where's Myna?" Satya asked, sitting down next to me.

"She went somewhere last night," I said, wisely.

"Oh, she told you?" Sahana asked.

I froze. I should've kept my mouth shut.

"No…" I said, but I didn't have to explain, because Myna appeared in a burst of light.

"Hey, guys," she said, without missing a beat, "Get dressed, we're going somewhere."

I could feel my face shining, "Where?"

"What's that?" Sahana asked, pointing at a fresh scar on Myna's arm.

"I fell," she said, trying to walk away.

"Where did you go?" Satya asked, sharply.

Myna sighed, "Satya, stop that."

"Stop what?" Shyamala asked, squinting her brows, "I feel out of the loop."

"I second that," I said, looking back and forth between Satya and Myna.

"Satya can tell when someone's lying," Myna explained, "It's a gift she got from her grandfather, the god of righteousness."

"Oh," I said, not focusing on Satya's superpower, "You lied?"

Satya snorted as Myna glared at her, "Yeah, I did. You don't need to know what I lied about, though."

"We *need* to know," Sahana said, "Right now. Or I'll die from curiosity."

She sidestepped towards her bow which lay by the couch, trying to make the point.

"Rohan burnt down the hotel," Myna said, "Probably as revenge for that little airplane incident. It's not a big deal."

"He burnt down a hotel!" I said, not trying to hide my shock.

"The one that we trained in?" Sahana asked.

"No, there's a bigger one in India," Myna said, nonchalantly.

She seemed chill about it, but there was panic in her voice when she found out last night.

"Go change quickly," Myna said, "Wear a *kurti*."

Amrita sighed and left with Sahana following her. Satya seemed to be too shocked to move.

I realized that she'd probably grown up there.

I didn't feel so excited to meet our mother anymore. I wanted to tell Satya that it was all a joke and the hotel was fine.

I walked to my room, my fists clenched. Rohan had burnt down a hotel!

And I was about to join him on that plane. I seethed in silence, sitting down on the bed.

Rohan called me "our queen" that day on the plane, but Sahana had said that Satya was the most likely candidate for the throne.

Something wasn't adding up.

SUBHADRAI

I THINK YOU'RE DUMB

"The greatest virtue is to bear insult without resentment." – Bhishma, Mahabharata

When we'd all changed, Myna *still* wouldn't tell us where we were going.

I kept pestering her for information, but she wouldn't spill. What if we weren't meeting Draupadi?

She made us binge watch a TV show about the Mahabharata for educational purposes, apparently.

It was really good until this scene where one of Arjuna's sons (so, Sahana's brother. That's so weird), Abhimanyu died. Then Shyamala started crying, and *I* started crying (because of the dust, obviously) and I doubted anyone had dry eyes after that.

At lunch when the five of us were sitting at the dining table, Myna came over to us and sat next to me looking exhausted.

"We're going to Panchalam," she said, putting a bunch of rice on her plate.

The name rang a bell from the show we'd watched that morning. I was pretty sure it was a kingdom.

"That's Draupadi's home," Amrita said, "Right?"

Satya nodded, "Yeah, it is."

"Draupadi is our mother," I confirmed.

Satya nodded, but Sahana looked confused.

"Wait, I missed that scene. Why is she the wife of all five of the Pandavas?" Sahana asked.

"Arjuna won Draupadi at a ceremony," Satya explained, "But when he went home, he told his mother he'd brought home a gift."

"Oh yeah!" I recalled, "Then their mother told Arjuna to share the gift! That's why she married all of them."

"They listened?" Sahana asked, her eyes wide.

"Yeah, back in the day, people actually listened to their elders," Satya laughed, "Hint, hint."

"Very funny," Amrita rolled her eyes, "But, Myna, Panchalam doesn't exist anymore."

Satya smirked as Myna blinked at her.

"What do you mean it doesn't exist anymore?"

"It's from the show, right?" Sahana asked.

Myna laughed, "Why does that imply that it's not real?"

Sahana looked at her as if it were obvious, "It's a *show*. Nothing in it is real."

"If nothing in it is real, then you wouldn't be either," Myna said, her face turning serious, "Do I have to remind you that you're the daughter of Arjuna and Draupadi?"

Sahana stared at her hands as if she hadn't seen them before. It even took a while for me to remember. Nothing still felt *real* yet.

Myna took this moment of silence as a chance to explain, "Ever since Brahma decided to restart the Mahabharata, ancient India's been forming again. This little underground palace is on the outskirts of the kingdom Indraprastha. If you recall, Indraprastha was originally the kingdom of the Pandavas."

"If it's the Pandavas' palace, then, why don't we stay there?" I asked.

"We're not allowed to enter the cities of Indraprastha or Hastinapura until a ruler is decided," Satya said, "Bhishma thinks staying in a kingdom will get to our heads."

"But then what about the people?" Sahana asked.

"The citizens' minds will be... *persuaded* by the gods to think that wherever Panchalam used to be eons ago is Panchalam once more. Indraprastha and Hastinapura are as real as you and me," Myna said.

"Wait, so whoever is ruling the kingdom *now* are the same rulers that were there during the Mahabharata?" Shyamala asked.

"No," Myna said, "Good question. The rulers who have been established are those who resemble the kingdom the best. For example, when you say Ayodhya, then Lord Rama will be the first person to come to your mind."

Lord Rama was an Indian god who used to rule the kingdom of Ayodhya. I remembered Amma telling me his story when Amrita and I were younger.

"Rama is back on Earth?" Amrita asked, shocked.

"Wait. No. That was a bad example. Since Rama is an incarnation of a god, he can't really reincarnate on Brahma's command. His *father* is ruling the kingdom," Myna said, "The cool thing is that the time gap between the Ramayana and Mahabharata is more than centuries apart. Kind of like *Lord of the Rings* meeting *Bluey*."

"I don't understand," Sahana frowned, "India isn't a democratic country anymore?"

Myna looked flustered, "Well yes… and no. It's basically a loose constitutional monarchy, where the monarchs have more power. If there *are* any rulers misusing their power, then the gods will strip them of it in one way or another."

"Ah…" I said, slowly, "So… when did this change even happen? I've been coming to India for summer vacation as long as I remember, and I never noticed."

"You have ancient blood in you, so you won't feel the spell Brahma cast on the others," Myna explained, "In a while though, even to you, it'll feel like we were always under monarchy."

"So… does that mean all the skyscrapers will be turned into huts now?" Sahana asked.

Myna hit her forehead, "Oh, yeah, sure. And we might as well turn all the phones into straw while we're at it, huh? *No!* It's basically modern ancient India."

"Modern and Ancient are antonyms," Amrita pointed out.

"Yes, well India is an oxymoron," Myna sighed.

"Did you call India a moron?" I asked, bewildered.

"No!" Myna said, angrily, "Don't you learn English?!"

"Nah, our English teacher retired, and our school is still looking for a new one," I grinned, "It's been that way for two years."

"Okay, listen. There were twenty-eight states in India originally. All of them are gone now, and they're replaced with the kingdoms that were in India during the medieval period," Myna said, "Still, though, everything else is the same. Everyone's still addicted to their phones. There's pollution everywhere. It's just a tiny difference in how the country is run."

Sure, tiny.

"Soo... The Kauravas are fighting to rule all of India?" I asked.

Satya answered for Myna this time, "No, the Kauravas want two kingdoms, Hastinapura and Indraprastha."

"Why?" Amrita asked.

"BECAUSE THEY DO!" Myna screamed, losing her cool.

"Okay, listen," Satya ordered, "They think it belongs to them being the direct descendants of the king. *We* are trying to stop them because the second oldest in the clan rightfully deserves to be queen. Rohan just wants to rule to impress his father."

All eyes turned to me as I made a weird choking sound.

"Wait me?" I asked.

"Yes, you!" Satya said, "You're the next queen, aren't you?"

"Huh," I looked around, bewildered, "Did all of you know this?"

They nodded.

I tried to find the right words to say that I couldn't rule a kingdom! I couldn't even get twenty kids to remember to write a math test!

"So… lemme get this straight," Sahana said before I could say anything, "India is now ruled by a monarchy and is split into different kingdoms. The Kauravas want two of these kingdoms, specifically Hastinapura and Indraprastha, because Rohan's grandfather was the king, and he is his direct descendant. The Pandavas don't want them to have it, because it doesn't follow the 'first born, first rule' thing, and not following it would break the law of righteousness or something."

"Why do *I* have to be queen?" I asked, ignoring Sahana.

"Because a prophecy told us that Satya wasn't destined to be queen, and the next child was! *We* think that the next child means you, and the Kauravas think the next child means the king's grandson, which means Rohan," Myna said, as if she'd said it a hundred times, "And if *you* don't want to, I suppose we could keep passing the responsibility down until we decide that Rohan should have it anyways."

I hesitated for a moment.

Queen. I liked the sound of that more than I could admit. I would do *anything* to prove I could rule.

But could I?

I thought of Rohan burning down the hotel. That was how he would rule a kingdom, killing anything in his way.

I suppose you're not cut out to be a leader after all.

I frowned. I *was* cut out to be a leader. I was cut out to be a *queen*.

"Right. No, I'm good," I said, "One more question."

"Go on," Myna sighed.

"Why do *we* have to fight? Our parents have done it before, so why don't they do it again?" I asked.

"Because Duryodhana doesn't want to be king, *Rohan* does," Myna cried, "And Draupadi doesn't want to be queen, *you* do, don't you?"

"Yeah," I decided, dropping the conversation.

****

When Amrita and Sahana walked into the hallway that evening I was waiting impatiently at the trapdoor eating a donut.

I'd gotten dressed as soon as possible, but, for some reason, nobody else seemed that excited to get to Panchalam.

If looks could kill, Amrita (who had walked into the room wearing a crumpled t-shirt) would have dropped dead in half a milli-second, but (fortunately for her) they can't.

Once all of the PD (The short form for Pandavas' Daughters for short that Myna had come up with that nickname because calling us by our names was a mouthful for her to keep repeating) had gathered into the room I swallowed the donut, "So, car or light-travel?"

Sahana jerked her head back and forth quickly, "NOT light-travel. I can't handle another one of Subhadrai's 'episodes'."

"Shut up, Khatri," I said, but light-traveling is *not* a part of my must-do-daily list.

I didn't even have a must-do-daily list.

After Satya and Sahana had found a car, we started our journey, like they say, with a step. Or in our case, an attempt at a step. I tripped on my shoelaces crashing into Satya who toppled onto Shyamala who pushed Amrita, who took the balance of Sahana.

Once we'd taken our second step, we boarded the car that Sahana had found.

"How'd you get the car?" I asked.

"I have my ways," she smirked.

"By 'her ways' she means she stole it from a gas station while the owner went shopping," Satya said.

Sahana frowned, "I didn't steal it, I *politely* asked the guy who was leaning on it if I could borrow the car, and he told me the keys were inside, so I could. And I paid too."

"That was a homeless dude," Satya sighed.

"Oh," Sahana said, embarrassed, "I couldn't tell, he was wearing a suit. Why didn't you tell me?"

Satya shrugged, "We were in a rush, and you left money anyways."

I stifled my laughter. The poor guy who actually owned the car was going to be so angry when he found out that this random guy let a 11-year-old borrow his car.

"Who's driving?" I asked.

"Satya, duh," Sahana said, with a chuckle, "She's the only one old enough."

"Oh, right," I nodded, "How old *are* you?"

"Eighteen," Satya said, slipping into the driver seat.

"You know, with all the war training, how much *driving* practice did you get?" Sahana asked, suspiciously.

"I skipped a lot of training for this," Satya said, proudly.

"You?" I asked, "The daughter of *Yudhishthira?*"

"Meh, no one's perfect," Satya said, starting the engine.

"Where do I sit?" I asked, peeking into the car through the window.

Satya turned to look at the filled-up seats, "Oh… How do you feel about sitting in the trunk?"

***

Panchalam is beautiful. It's gorgeous, it's lovely, it's absolutely terrible. The second we walked into the palace garden; a ball hit Sahana's face.

"ALL RIGHT!" she screamed, "WHICH DOOFUS DID THAT?"

"Watch who you're talking to," a guy said, walking towards us, his hand outstretched for the ball, "We're pretty high authority, newbie."

"In your *dreams*," Sahana retorted, tossing the ball at his face instead of his outstretched hand.

He stared at her in shock. I was shocked too. Sahana had always seemed a lot more… peaceful?

The boy's younger brother walked up towards us and straightened his glasses.

He cocked his eyebrows, looking unnaturally like… me.

The boy whose face Sahana had hit scowled at me. An expression we knew all too well. She realized with a sigh that she'd hit Satya's brother.

"Well, *we*," Sahana smirked, probably ignoring that fact, "are *higher* authority."

"We are?" Shyamala said, leaning towards her.

"Yes," Sahana snapped, "And obviously, we're *so* much better."

We were. We were dressed in traditional Indian *Kurtis,* and they were wearing … Well, it wasn't anywhere close to "high authority".

"Uh…You can only be high authority of *this* palace if you're a daughter of Draupadi, so if you happen to be a daughter of the Pandavas but not Draupadi then you're *not* high authority, idiot," the boy with glasses said.

What he meant was that even though all the Pandavas were married to Draupadi, they had wives of their own too. It was normal to have more than one wife, back in the day.

"We're children of Draupadi," I said, stepping up, and the closer I got to him the more obvious it was to see that I was older than the male version of me.

"No, you're not," said the boy with glasses.

"Oh really?" I asked.

Shyamala looked back and forth between us. I looked so much like glasses-boy, it was impossible *not* to notice.

"I think someone duped you," said Satya's brother.

"*I* think you're dumb," Sahana said, which was not a proper comeback, but it's all we had at the moment.

The boy opened his mouth, probably to point that out, but I sighed, loudly.

"Are you guys stupid?" I gestured to myself, "Look at me and look at you."

Satya's brother looked back and forth between me and glasses-boy.

"She's right, dude," he stage-whispered.

That's when Satya walked in, and grinned, "Hey guys. Say 'hi' to your sisters."

Satya's brother rolled his eyes, "Not *you*. I thought you left to America for good," he turned to me, "I'm Prathivindhya and you can call me Prath. This is Sutasoma and you cannot call him Sut."

I shook his hand, and he gave Sahana a nod.

"Come on in," Sutasoma muttered.

The two boys led us to the palace which (I don't know if I mentioned) in all honesty was really, beautiful.

As we were walking, something clicked in my mind. If these children of the Pandavas were alive, then would that mean…. Abhimanyu was alive! I supposed he wouldn't be in Panchalam, (Draupadi isn't his mother), but maybe in Dwaraka, which was *his* mother's kingdom.

After that, I recalled how we'd all started sobbing when Abhimanyu died, and decided that if we ever did cross paths, we'd never, ever mention that. I made a mental note to fill Sahana in on this.

Once we entered the room, an arrow whizzed past Sahana's face nearly giving me a heart attack.

"Oh," said a boy with an impish smile, "I thought you were Sutasoma…Who *are* you?"

I ignored him, focusing on the throne where an old man sat, staring at us angrily.

"*Girls*," he muttered resentfully, eyeing his ring, "You're welcome to drop by Panchalam anytime you want after telling us at three in the morning. Oh wait, no. You're not."

I thought Draupadi *invited* us. I don't think anyone filled this person in.

"What a nice guy," Sahana muttered.

"Lighten up," said the boy, "On the bright side, he can throw you in prison and torture you until you die."

She glared at him, as he stuck his tongue out at her.

"SHRUTAKARMA!" screeched a lady's voice, "I TOLD YOU TO CLEAN YOUR ROOM! IF YOU'RE STILL TRYING TO SCARE YOUR BROTHERS THEN-"

A lady had walked into the room, and she stopped screaming once she saw us.

I glanced at her then at everyone else in the room. I couldn't help but notice that her eyes seemed awfully familiar.

The lady smiled, "Oh, thank goodness you're here. Now *someone* can show Shrutakarma here how to behave."

She gestured to the idiot named Shrutakarma who'd nearly given me a heart attack.

Sahana grinned, "Don't worry, I've already started."

I studied the lady. It was most definitely the lady in the picture. She looked maybe eighteen years old, but that couldn't be right. Her black hair fell across her right shoulder in a long (very long) plait. Her red saree was encrusted in diamonds, I wondered how she even felt comfortable in it. Nestled against her bronze skin was a ruby necklace.

"Do I get an introduction?" asked the man on the throne.

"Oh yes," the lady smiled, and it seemed like she was looking at me, "That's my father, King Drupada."

Two men appeared from a tall arched doorway discussing something urgently. The tallest one had deep brown eyes that seemed to hold the wisdom of centuries, like Satya's. The next guy was a bit shorter and was trying to peek into the phone the taller man held.

"Draupadi," he called in a voice that seemed silkier than his hair, "What's the Wi-Fi password?"

It *was* Draupadi! I bounced up and down on my toes.

Draupadi sighed, "Seriously, Arjuna. Again?"

I nearly squealed. That was Sahana's father!

I glanced at Sahana who pursed her lips. She shrunk away behind me as a burly man walked in, wiping his mouth.

"Yo, Arjuna! Did you taste that *kheer* in the kitchen?" his eyes sparkled with excitement, "I hope you did, because I had the whole pot."

"Draupadi, we really need that password," Arjuna said, "Sahadeva foresaw the future, and posted it on Instagram, and we need to delete that right now."

Two identical men ran in, in panic, and the one with a beard screamed, "Did you delete it?!"

"Meet Yudhishthira, Bhima, Arjuna, Nakula and Sahadeva," Draupadi sighed.

"That's the password?" Yudhishthira said, looking up.

He stared at us for a second, then nudged Arjuna. All five of them turned to look at us, their faces in total confusion.

Draupadi turned towards them and mouthed something, but they obviously didn't get it.

"Welcome back," said the burly man.

Draupadi slapped her forehead.

I realized with a jolt who it was. I felt my heartbeat quicken as I tried to calm my breath. I was in front of my father. My *actual* father.

"That's Bhima," I heard Sahana tell Amrita confirming my suspicion.

'Back?' Amrita asked, 'It's our first time here.'

Bhima blinked, "Really? I thought-'

The eldest, Yudhishthira, Satya's dad, quickly intervened, 'No, you're talking about those other kids.'

Bhima frowned, 'No, I don't thi-'

'Oh my *god*, Bhima,' said Arjuna, 'Catch on, would you?'

Satya glared at the five brothers as she walked in, and Sahana, Shyamala, Amrita and I blinked at the Pandavas in confusion.

Bhima slowly nodded, 'Right. I think I was talking about those other kids.'

'Which one is mine?' Arjuna asked, curiously.

Sahana hesitantly raised her hand from behind me.

Arjuna frowned, 'Ah… are you good at archery?' he asked, because that's the first question that every dad asks when they see their daughters for the first time.

"Yes," she said (and that wasn't a lie), "but *that* guy sucks at it."

She pointed at the one named Shrutakarma who'd tried to scare us.

"HOW WOULD YOU KNOW THAT?" Shrutakarma roared.

"You *look* like you're bad at archery," She frowned, "Plus, you never scared us with your terrible shot."

Okay, he did, but that's between you and me.

Arjuna shook his head and looked at Sahana with a grin, "Tell me about it."

Sahana grinned and I realized this family meeting wouldn't be so hard after all.

***

In a few minutes, the sons of the last two Pandavas arrived, Satanika and Shrutasena. I congratulate the person who came up with these names, by the way.

Amrita and Satanika seemed to get along well, but something told me Shrutasena wasn't much of a talker.

We sat down for dinner, and so that we could "bond", we had to sit next to our brothers. Bhima would've been proud of the way Shrutakarma stuffed his food in his mouth.

"Manners," Sahana muttered.

"What?" he asked.

"Manners. Where are your manners?" she snapped.

"What are those?" Shrutakarma said, his face serious.

She blinked at him, shocked.

Obviously, English wasn't our mother tongue. Sanskrit was. But I think that Shrutakarma question completely changed the way I thought about people in ancient times. But hey, at least we didn't brush our teeth with urine (No offense. I love Rome).

"What are those?" Shrutakarma repeated.

"They're..." Sahana paused; *how do you explain manners?*

"Yeah?" Shrutakarma asked, raising his eyebrows.

"Satya?" Sahana asked.

"Yes," Satya said, leaning forward to look at them.

"What is the meaning of manners?" Sahana asked.

Satya took out her phone and searched it up.

"It means, 'a person's outward bearing or way of behaving towards others'," Satya said.

"Ah," Shrutakarma said, turning to Sahana, "Because that makes perfect sense."

"What *doesn't* make sense?" she asked.

"You asked, "Where are your *a person's outward bearing or way of behaving towards others?*" He smirked.

I was shocked that he actually remembered that.

"I said, 'Where is your polite outward behavior?'" Sahana snapped.

"With me," Shrutakarma said, "Why?"

"Never mind," Sahana muttered, and let him eat the way he was.

"Just saying," he said, when we were done, "I was pulling your leg. I know what manners are."

She looked up at him as he walked away, "I hate you!"

Sutasoma grinned, "I thought I was the only one."

"Harr harr," Prativindhya muttered, "We all hate him."

"Talking about me?" Shrutakarma asked walking back in, "I'm irresistible, aren't I?"

He picked his phone up off the table and walked away leaving everyone to bury their faces in their hands.

Shrutakarma popped his head back in the room grinning "By the way, I'm still amazing even if you hate me. No one can beat *me*!"

And he slid back to where he came from.

I rolled my eyes. In the original Mahabharata, Ashwattama, an old classmate of the Pandavas, sort of *killed* him...I think that counts as a defeat.

SUBHADRAI

KIDS THESE DAYS

"The mind is restless and difficult to restrain, but it can be controlled through practice and detachment." – Lord Krishna, Bhagavad Gita

I was happy that Bhima and Sutasoma were fine with me. We'd spoken for a while after dinner, and I know that I shouldn't care what they think either way, but it was still reassuring that they didn't want me to die.

Sahana obviously disliked Shrutakarma. I started to get annoyed with him too when he took us on a tour of the palace. Half the puns he made were *so* reused.

I stared at the halls, thinking that they looked sort of familiar, but my déjà vu was interrupted by Shrutakarma crude imitations of a fart, which has been getting way too popular recently. For mankind's sake I hope that the person who figured out you could make farts with your armpits gets some punishment.

Anyways, putting aside Shrutakarma's farting armpit, the palace was really cool. Still, Sahana and I talked about it later and the kingdom felt way too familiar. I felt like I'd been here before.

Eventually we came across a room marked "*BAALIKAA*", which Satya told me was the Sanskrit word for *girl*.

"Who's staying here?" I asked.

"Oh," Draupadi said, "The five of you will sleep here, and the boys will be in the next room."

"Speaking of which," Yudhishthira said, "You kids should get to bed."

Sahadeva frowned but nodded.

Sahadeva was famous for telling the future (which was the reason they needed the Wi-Fi password when we came. I wondered if he ever got it), so Amrita took that as an excuse.

"Sahadeva frowned," Amrita said.

"So?" Yudhishthira asked.

"Well, he must have had some deep revelation on how you shouldn't send us to bed now...," Amrita prompted, "You know, because he can tell the future-"

"Go to bed," Sahadeva laughed.

She scowled and sulked off into the room and the rest of us followed. It took a million centuries for me to fall asleep (okay, one hour), and unfortunately, I woke up in the middle of the night, at around two fifteen to screams of fright.

"What is going *on*?" I muttered.

I heard a scream coming from the boys' area, "GET OFF OF ME! GET OFF! GEROFF!"

My eyes immediately widened. Satya and Amrita also got up.

The three of us rushed towards the room, and I swear I saw Sahana open her eyes and then close them again when she heard the voice. I thought for a moment and then recognized it too… It belonged to Shrutakarma. I was tempted to stop in my tracks, but I decided against it. As annoying as he was, it sounded like he was in trouble.

We rushed into the room to see Prath, Sutasoma, Satanika, and Shrutasena. Who we did not see was Shrutakarma.

"He was kidnapped," Prathivindhya explained.

"By a girl," Sutasoma said, wide-eyed.

Sahadeva tried to say something, but decided not to.

Satya scowled at Sutasoma but pushed past him walking towards the balcony where Arjuna stood.

"Crime in this kingdom is low as it is," Arjuna growled at the guards, "If it happens once in a million years, can't you stop it?"

"Sorry sir, the lady was too quick," the guards muttered knowing it was useless, and that they were probably going to get fired.

Arjuna saw us and told the guards to step back, "I need your help."

"Excuse me?" I raised my eyebrows.

"You need to find Shrutakarma," Arjuna said seriously.

"Excuse me?" I asked again, "Why us? Why not them?"

I pointed at the guys who pushed my hand away as Sahana walked in.

"I don't know," Arjuna shrugged, "If you're going to be in charge of the kingdom, I assumed you'd take the initiative to SAVE YOUR BROTHER!"

I suppose you're not cut out to be a leader after all.

I took a deep breath, trying to calm myself. I wasn't sure if I wanted to scream or cry, but I *wasn't* wasting precious time I could be using to train, looking for some idiot who thinks he can't be beat.

Sahana raised an eyebrow, "Um, no."

I nodded, "Yeah, we hardly know-"

Arjuna scowled as Draupadi ran in.

"What is going on?!" Draupadi asked, as close to frustration as she could possibly dare to get.

"They said that it was our job to go get him," Sutasoma scowled, "I mean as if-"

"Shrutakarma got himself kidnapped," Satya said, cutting to the point.

Draupadi immediately counted the boys and ended up with four.

"Nice prank," she scowled, "Where is he?"

"He was kidnapped," Prathivindhya promised, "Would I lie?"

Draupadi stared at the son of Yudhishthira. Yudhishthira was the son of the god of righteousness, famous for never telling a lie, so it was *very* unlikely that Prathivindhya, the son of Yudhishthira would lie.

"Fine," Draupadi said, calmly, "Do you know who did it?"

"It was a lady," Shrutasena, the son of Sahadeva explained, "And she had the Magadha royal emblem on her cloak."

Draupadi frowned, "The kingdom of Magadha is on the Kauravas' side. I didn't think they would go *this* far."

"That Rohan dude is a jerk," Prathivindhya scowled, "Once when we were playing cricket, he-"

"Shut up," Draupadi turned to Sahadeva's son, "Are you sure she was from Magadha? It's not Ambika?"

He shook his head, "No, she had dark black hair too."

I frowned. Who was Ambika?

Whatever. I wasn't going all the way to *Magadha* to find Shrutakarma, wherever that was.

"Also," Arjuna said, "You can't light-travel to Magadha. It can be tracked. We can't let anyone find you and take you too."

The four of us were about to complain but Satya stopped us, "Okay."

Once Arjuna and Draupadi had left, Satya turned to us, "Get some sleep. Don't argue, we're leaving tomorrow. I'll explain later."

When we got to our room, Satya turned to me, "We should go look for him?"

"Why?" I complained.

"He's our brother, and that's what family does," Satya said, "But also, Arjuna wants us to look for him to prove that we're capable of, you know, ruling. Specifically, you, Subhadrai."

I looked at Satya skeptically. No way…

"Just do it, Subhadrai," Satya said, "Don't worry about training. You'll get plenty of practice during the trip."

I sighed. If this is what it took to sit on that throne, then…

"Fine."

The next day, I followed Satya into the dining room with the others.

The second I walked in, Shyamala stood up in shock and Amrita followed.

Satya stared at them curiously, "Guys, eat."

"About time you were alone," said Shyamala in a voice that did not belong to her.

I've watched enough of Amrita's wacko movies to know that when somebody starts talking in a voice that doesn't belong to them, there's no other explanation. They've obviously been possessed by some ancient spirit or something.

"Who are you?" Sahana said, standing up.

She must have watched those movies too.

Amrita had watched those movies too, so she followed the protocol, letting out a gentle laugh, *"I am Asti, the princess of Magadha."*

Asti was the daughter of the king of Magadha and the wife of the king of Mathura, another powerful kingdom on the Kauravas' side. I'd never been so shocked. I nearly had a heart attack.

Satya stared in shock, "Asti? But... you're... You're Kamsa's wife!"

Kamsa was the king of Mathura. He was the most ruthless king in history. Take the world's worst tyrant, multiply him by ten, put it into one person and you get an accurate description of Kamsa. Though he's probably worse than that. He tried to kill his sister on her *wedding* day! It took a god to kill him last time.

Kamsa had two wives; Asti and Prapti.

The gods had reinstated the stupid oaf as a king! Of course! He *was* the first thing I thought of when I thought of Mathura.

"Yes," Amrita/Asti said, *"I have your brother. But to find him, you do need help, don't you? I can't tell you outright, but I don't want to hold him hostage. I can give you a clue."*

"Wait," Sahana said, "You're helping us?"

"Yes," Shyamala said, politely, *"Please shut up for some time and listen. I need some help from you. You need to get to Mathura soon and free two kids, a girl and a boy, from my husband's prison. (How you do it is not my problem.) Once you do that, you need to come to Magadha and get your brother. Your reward for this little favor will be given to you through a friend of mine. Listen to him, okay?"*

Amrita shuddered and blinked, "Wh-What happened?"

Asti had left. How had she possessed her though?

I opened my mouth and tried to explain. Instead, I gestured to Sahana to do the honors. She stared at Amrita, open-mouthed.

"Truth is," Sahana said, "I don't know."

"It's not that big of a deal. At least she didn't foresee something," Satya sighed, "Last year, my father was possessed like that by a man. He's the one who told us that 'the next' should rule the kingdom. We have to listen to them, so I guess we're taking a detour to Mathura, because *I'm* not ignoring that."

****

The next morning, we were parked in a gas station near Mathura trying to figure out a plan. We'd taken the homeless dude's car again, but this time, I sat in the shotgun.

"Did she mention *why* those two kids were in jail?" Amrita asked.

I shook my head.

"What if we're helping someone evil bust out of jail?" Amrita said, "What if Asti is working for Rohan?"

"She *is* working for Rohan," I laughed, "That's why she captured Shrutakarma!"

"Then, why are we doing this?" Amrita asked.

"Because Satya thinks that Kamsa only imprisons good people, and it's worth a try," I said.

This was true, though. Kamsa *only* imprisoned good people. People like his father, his newlywed sister and her husband.

He's a nice guy like that.

After that conversation Sahana decided that we were going to wing it by pretending we were important royals who needed to get into the palace prison for no specific reason.

Great plan, right?

In our defense, we were exhausted and didn't really care if it worked out or not. Seven hours in the car can drive a person mad.

We stayed the night in the car (don't ask, it was terrible), and the next morning we walked towards the kingdom, which was a five-minute walk from the gas station, leaving our car for any homeless dude who might want to lend it to another group of kids.

Once we reached the palace, we realized we didn't need to get in to find the prison. The whole palace was surrounded by cages filled with innocent-looking people.

It didn't take me long to find the kids though. There were only two outside, a girl and a boy in a small cage. Outside the cage were two burly guards.

Satya seemed convinced that they were the kids we were looking for because they looked familiar to her.

The kids looked like how any other kids would look after being trapped in a cage; bored.

"How are we going to get them out?" I asked, turning to Amrita.

She shrugged, "We *could* create a distraction."

Satya sighed, "What could you possibly do to distract them?"

"Um, well, I could scream, '*AH! OH MY GOD!! I'M ON FIRE!!!*'," Sahana said, waving her hands in the air, rolling her eyes.

At once, all eyes were on us.

"*Now* what?" I hissed, exasperated.

We didn't need to worry about what happened next though because that's when the king, Kamsa, stepped out onto his balcony, and everyone else frantically resumed their work, which was constructing a giant-size statue of Kamsa.

It didn't take the king long to spot a group of girls on his palace ground squabbling instead of working. I watched as he whispered to his guard and pointed at us.

In another minute, a few soldiers walked towards us dragging another cage with them.

"Uh, guys," I said, tapping Sahana on the shoulder, "Right now may be a good time to quit arguing."

"What?!" Amrita frowned, exasperated.

I pointed at the cage nearing us flanked by three soldiers on each side, "We're kinda, sorta in serious trouble."

Satya hit her forehead with the base of her palm, "Couldn't you have mentioned that earlier?"

One of the soldiers who were guarding the kids' cage turned around and unlocked the door. They grabbed the kids by the scruff of their necks and led them to the construction site.

The soldier coming for us pulled out a sword from his belt and brandished it, "Stay put!"

I watched as the kids were left near the statue, unguarded and free to be taken away by us.

"We'll run to the kids on the count of three and we'll light-travel away," I whispered to Satya, ignoring Arjuna's instructions to not light-travel.

"One," I whispered, as Satya told the rest of the group.

"Two."

The soldier walked past the kids' cage towards us and pulled out a handcuff.

"THREE!"

We broke out into a run towards the kids. Amrita reached first and quickly filled them in on what we were about to do. The girl then made some odd gestures with her hand and the boy nodded.

By the time I reached, Amrita had discovered something scary.

"I can't light-travel," she said.

I tried, but it didn't work for me either.

"Satya?" I asked, panic building up in my throat.'

"There must be a block," she said, "Some kingdoms have a ban on light-travel. I wouldn't be surprised if Kamsa's kingdom did too."

"Oh golly," I said, "It would have killed you to mention this possibility before we ran away from six ripped soldiers who wanted to lock us in a cage, wouldn't it?"

Satya shrugged feebly, "Well, *you* didn't tell me about the soldiers. I forgot."

She turned to look at the kids and then at the soldier (who was whispering something to his pals), then quickly back at the kids.

"Wait a sec," she gasped, "I know you!"

"Yeah!" said the girl, "You're Yudhishthira's daughter!"

"Yes!" Satya laughed, "Guys, these are *Arjuna's* kids! The girl is Akshara, and the boy is Vedanth!"

"Wow, great," Sahana said, "I'm an Arjuna kid, too, it's not a big deal. Unfortunately, that doesn't really change anything and we're still about to be captured."

The soldiers started walking again, but this time it was a bit faster.

"Why don't they run?" I wondered aloud.

"Their armor is too heavy," Akshara laughed, 'Trust me, I know.'

The boy did an odd hand action and Akshara laughed, "Yeah! I remember!"

"He's deaf," Amrita whispered to me.

"Oh," I nodded.

I turned around and to my horror found that the soldiers were only a few more paces away from us, swords drawn and terribly angry.

"Somebody, come up with a plan!" I said, looking back at the group.

Vedanth signed something to his sister.

"What's he saying?!" I asked.

Akshara opened her mouth, but then the soldier screamed something about us staying put again.

"Well?" Shyamala asked, inching closer to us away from the soldiers.

"Vedanth told us to run."

That's when King Kamsa came out of the kingdom and glared at us.

ROHAN

GREAT IDEA

"What is a greater happiness to a father than what the father feels when his son, running to him, clasps him with his tiny little arms, though his body is full of dust and dirt." - Mahabharata

I stuffed the last piece of my peanut butter and jelly into my mouth and looked up at my mother, Bhanumati.

She didn't look too impressed about my record-breaking consumption of the sandwich. On the other hand, she looked quite disappointed.

"What's wrong?" I asked.

"He's your *friend!*" she said, dropping another sandwich onto my plate.

"I'm not hungry," I said, "Did Ambika already eat?"

"Your sister's in the veranda with Nisata," Bhanumati said, "They're sword fighting. I don't think she's eaten yet."

"Does dad know?" I asked, standing up.

"Of course not," Bhanumati laughed, "But she won't eat it, and I doubt anybody else will. I don't understand how you enjoy this!"

With a sigh, I picked up the PB&J, sitting down again.

"He's your friend, Rohan," Bhanumati said again, ruffling my hair, "You can't do this to him!"

"I'm sure the other boys will be happy," I said, "I was doing them a favor. Plus, they're not my friends."

"Shrutakarma is *still* their brother," Bhanumati said, "The girls have already gone looking for him."

"How'd you find that out?" I asked, looking up.

"Asti told me. She called me this morning."

"How would Asti know?"

There was a gap of silence, and I turned to look at my mother who stood behind me, with a confused expression.

"I didn't ask."

"Rohan, m'boy!" came a booming voice from the entrance of the dining hall, 'Great idea!'

My head snapped towards my father who'd walked in. He wore baggy shorts, a dark gray T-shirt and headphones were hanging from his neck.

"How was your walk?" Bhanumati asked, leaning on my chair.

"Good, good," Duryodhana said with a smile, "I spoke to Jarasandha. He told me all about your idea!"

He smiled and patted me on the back making a thousand fireworks go off in my chest.

"That Shrutakarma is Arjuna's son, right?" Duryodhana asked.

I nodded.

"How did you kidnap him?" Duryodhana asked, curiously.

"I asked Asti Aunty to light-travel into the room," I said "Because, you know, she's part of the council."

The council was a group of people carefully selected by the devas. I didn't know much about them, except three things: They could block people from light-traveling. They could travel through light-travel blocks placed on palaces (Like Panchalam) and they could vaguely tell the future.

So, I had Asti light-travel into the Pandavas' sons' room and take any random guy. Then I told her to place a light-travel block on any Pandava child who left the palace in the twenty-four hours that followed for two weeks. Which meant that even if a child of the Pandavas went outside right now, they'd have a block on them, so it wasn't really the most fool-proof plan, but even if the girls went after their brother, it would take them a while to find him.

And in that time, I could grow my army.

I told my father this, and he glanced at Bhanumati with a grin, "Can you believe this kid?"

He punched my shoulder with a laugh.

Bhanumati pursed her lips, because I was pretty sure she didn't consider "kidnapping your cousin" as something to be proud of.

It then dawned on Duryodhana that someone was missing.

"Where's Ambika?" he asked, sternly.

I glanced at my mother who glanced at me.

"She's with Viji," Bhanumati said, referring to Ambika's maid, "They're playing a game."

Not entirely a lie. Viji was probably with Ambika, and I guess fencing is a game, if you think about it.

Duryodhana seemed to consider the possibility, "The *boy* is not here, right?"

Bhanumati tensed, "Which one?"

"The one from Dwarka. Krishna's son," Duryodhana said.

Oh, that guy. He hadn't come here in ages. I was pretty sure he'd moved to London.

"No, he's been banned from the palace," Bhanumati reminded him.

"Oh, yes," Duryodhana remembered. "Call her. She should eat."

Bhanumati swiftly left as Duryodhana went to check what the cook had prepared. As he left, I heard new footsteps.

I turned around and saw a servant heading towards me.

"Sir," he said, his voice suspicious, "Your granduncle wishes to speak to you."

SUBHADRAI

RUN, RUN, RUN, RUN, RUN

"To deliver the pious and to annihilate the miscreants, I appear, millennium after millennium." – Lord Krishna, Bhagavad Gita

I'm giving you some advice here. Just, you know, engrave it into your brain or something. When an evil king (who killed his own citizens for fun and nearly killed his newly wed sister) comes running towards you, please don't stand there and say hi. Please, please run away.

Thank you.

"Run, run, run, run, run, run, run, run, run, run, run, run!" Akshara screamed, already running herself.

As if we weren't. All of us were running towards… Well, I don't know where we were running. Anywhere away from Kamsa was fine with me.

"CAVE!" Sahana said, pointing towards a rocky structure a few meters away.

Why is it that when people are running away, they *always* find a cave?

We kept running, nearer and nearer to the cave as Kamsa got closer to us. The wind picked up which oddly made it easier to run. I wasn't even panting as hard as everyone else was.

Just in time the wind started blowing harder. As if I didn't already feel like I was in a movie.

I felt myself moving swiftly through it. Only after Amrita told me did I realize why. My grandfather was the *god* of wind.

That was when I realized that Kamsa was two inches away from me. I yelped and tried to run even faster.

"Go!" Satya screamed, picking up a rock and throwing it at Kamsa's forehead.

We ran inside the cave and Kamsa's toe got in there too, but I stumbled and fell against the wall. The impact of a Bhima kid made the ceiling crumble, blocking the entrance.

"That," I said, faintly hearing Kamsa's cursing, "Was horrible. I need to rest for twelve-months."

"Not available," Sahana sighed, "We got to get out of here as soon as he leaves. We have an idiot to find."

"We're not getting out of here soon," I said, gesturing to the pile of rocks blocking us from exiting, "And it's not long before he finds a way in."

"Well then, I guess we could all exchange life stories," Sahana said, sarcastically, "You know, while we wait to die."

Satya smiled, "Okay, why not? The biggest turn in *my* life happened around eleven years ago. Draupadi had given birth to Sahana and Duryodhana's wife, Bhanumati, had given birth to their second child, Ambika. Around this time the Pandavas and Kauravas were friends, remember?"

"Right," I remembered, "What happened after that. Why were you the only girl raised in India?"

"Good question," Satya said, proudly, "You probably know that monarchy follows the first born, first rule thing. Since I was the eldest, the plan was to send the four of you to the USA along with Rohan's sister. The boys would be trained for the army, so they weren't sent away. To avoid jealousy, Draupadi sent the lot of you to different parts of the world to be taken care of handpicked loyal friends. Bhanumati was supposed to do the same, but Duryodhana decided to train Rohan for kingship. Proof that not even rebirth can drain desire out of his mind."

So I had lived in the Panchalam palace for a while… No wonder it seemed so familiar.

"But you're not becoming queen," Amrita said.

"Yeah," Satya said, "Back to the story. Years passed and finally at a council meeting last year, the Pandavas revealed to me that I was going to become queen. That's when Yudhishthira was possessed and spoke the prophecy which said that I would not become queen and the next heir would rule instead. The Pandavas took it as the next by age, which is Subhadrai. Duryodhana took it as the next in line, and since Duryodhana's father was still king, that would mean Rohan. He revealed that he had been training Rohan to rule ever since he could walk. This angered the Pandavas because it was already agreed Rohan wouldn't be king. Duryodhana argued saying that Rohan was completely capable of ruling once he came of age."

"Wait, so that's why we're fighting?" Shyamala asked over the screaming from outside the cave, "Because Rohan was being trained."

"No," Satya said, shaking my head, "I told you. We couldn't decide who becomes the next ruler. That's why we're fighting. Well, actually we only go to war if Grandsire Bhishma, the eldest in our family, calls it, but both Duryodhana and my father have declared war.

There was silence.

Then I spoke, "So, who's *supposed* to rule. Me or Rohan?"

Satya flinched as if she was hoping I wouldn't ask that.

"You."

That's when the wall of rocks blocking the entrance tumbled down revealing four guys standing in front of Kamsa's dead body.

"Hey," said Prathivindhya, pulling the sword out of Kamsa's corpse, "Coming?"

"What are you doing here?" Satya asked, bewildered.

Prathivindhya shrugged, "Well, normally when your brother is kidnapped you want to find him."

"You said you didn't want to come," I said.

"We decided to help," Sutasoma shrugged, "We know you can do it, but… I mean, he's our brother too."

"We didn't think you could do it," Prathivindhya said, bluntly.

"What day is it?" I asked, ignoring him.

"The day after you left, drama queen," Sutasoma said, rolling his eyes.

Of course. I knew that.

Satya breathed in relief looking at Kamsa, "We should keep going."

"Where to?" Satanika asked, "I forgot. I was hardly awake."

"How did you end up here, then?' Amrita asked.

"We asked around. We have a friend named Nisata. He told us that he'd seen you guys from the palace windows," Prathivindhya said, "So we light-traveled here. Then we saw a huge army and Kamsa screaming at a few people and we figured it might be worth checking out."

"How heroic," Sahana rolled her eyes, "We're going to Magadha."

"You can light-travel?" I asked.

"Yes…," Satanika said slowly, "You can't?"

"No," Shyamala said, "not since we set off."

Prathivindhya attempted to light-travel but failed to.

"No!" Satanika groaned, "Not by foot."

ROHAN

THE WEIRD UNCLE GUY

"Nobody is nobody's friend, nobody is nobody's well-wisher, people become friends or enemies only from motives of interest," - Bhishma, Mahabharata

For a few days, I tossed the idea back and forth. Should I go speak to him or not? They *had* put my granduncle in the slammer for a reason. He was the sole reason for the original Mahabharata, twisting my father's mind for revenge against grandsire Bhishma.

He was imprisoned the second we discovered his existence.

If I went and spoke to him, his plans would secure an even higher chance of making my father proud. But on the other hand, Duryodhana would probably be disgusted if I took the advice of a creep like his uncle.

That day, though, I decided to go meet him. He'd talk his talk, and I could choose whether I would listen or not. If I did then he probably would've given me a good idea. If not, then I'd have to do with my own ideas.

I had planned to go at 12:30, but lunch that day took longer than I expected.

"You did, what?!" Duryodhana asked, his eyes nearly popping out of their sockets.

My sister had a huge gash running down her arm, and obviously Duryodhana couldn't care less about that. He was only worried about where she'd gotten it from.

"Let it go," Bhanumati said, as the palace doctor hurried in to treat the wound, "She won't do it again."

"That's what you said when she got this," Duryodhana pointed at a tiny scar on my sister's head.

I opened my mouth to ask if I could leave, but then the doctor put something on the gash, making my sister yelp.

"Sword fighting!" Duryodhana exclaimed, in fury, "That's not *your* job. That's Rohan's."

She glared at him.

"You know what? I can't keep you here anymore," Duryodhana said, "I'm sending you away."

"Duryodhana!" Bhanumati exclaimed.

"You argue, and you'll go too! There's a house in a nearby forest," he said, "I'll send you there. You'll have no weapons to use."

"Dad," I said, breaking the silence, "Can I leave?"

He poked his potato slices furiously and shook his head in a way I hoped was a nod. I stood up, and quickly walked outside towards the stables.

I hopped onto my mare and sped out the palace gates.

I was going to meet my grand uncle, Shakuni.

***

The wind rippled through my hair as I sped past the town towards the prison which stood at the edge of town in a dark, stony building. The typical prison any kingdom would have.

I stopped the horse outside the prison and tied it to the pillar. As I walked in, the guards gave me a salute, making me grin, because nothing felt better than a salute.

I made my way to the back of the prison where my father kept Shakuni.

Shakuni had planned the entire war out, step-by-step, and in the end, he'd won too. He may have died, but his goal was to ruin our clan.

From the war he started, he'd done exactly that.

I think that's the main reason my dad didn't fight the Pandavas for ten years, but then when they said I couldn't rule even though Satya wasn't going to, he got irritated.

Subhadrai hadn't even been trained, but I had.

Still, he was ordered by Bhishma to cease training me.

It didn't take me long to find Shakuni. His cell was the one with ten guards outside it. The odd part was that they were all standing a few feet away from the cell.

"Why're you standing so far away from him?" I asked one of the guards.

I glanced at the shriveled man in the cell. He didn't look so dangerous.

The guard looked at me, curiously, "You shouldn't be here, your majesty."

"Well, I am."

Who was *he* to tell me what to do?

"He knows how to twist your mind, sir," the guard said, a tone of caution in his voice, "He'll kill you from the inside."

I frowned at him. Talk about a drama queen.

I pushed past him and walked over to the old man in the cell. He looked up at me and smiled, proudly showcasing his rotten teeth.

"Rohan!" he exclaimed, "You look exactly like your father."

Ew.

"You called?" I asked, raising an eyebrow.

It was a gesture I sincerely hoped was more intimidating than hilarious. Once I'd done it to Ambika. The scars of humiliation will never leave me.

"Yes, yes," Shakuni nodded, "I was speaking with some of the other guys here. You want to be king, eh?"

"Yeah."

"Then don't do what your father did. Fate will always be on the Pandavas' side," Shakuni said with a scowl, "You need more than weapons. You need the Syamantaka gem."

I stared at him for a beat.

"Huh?" I asked, unimpressed.

I honestly expected him to say something useful. The Syamantaka gem was a powerful gem that gave the owner money if they were good and cursed them if they were bad. It was sort of like a toned-down version of the amulet from Sofia the First.

"Listen to me," Shakuni said, "The curse won't affect you. The gem is hidden in a key. The key will stop the gem from placing a curse, but if it leaves the gem, your curse may not be so bad after all."

"What do you mean?"

"As far as I know, you'll be granted power to kill more people. I don't really understand how that's a curse, though. Plus, the sun god added one more perk to the gem."

"That is?"

"If you stick the key into the war field, it'll raise an army of its own. Worth two *akshauhinis*. If you say no to this, lad, you are no more than a fool."

An akshauhini was a large part of an army.

I looked at the old man in the cell. He'd been there since his mid-twenties. It would be enough to drive a man mad, right?

It was shocking that Shakuni hadn't been affected. Or maybe he had…

I decided to play with the idea of finding the gem later, and without a word, left the prison in time to hear Shakuni say, "It *would* make your father proud!"

SUBHADRAI

TIME TO GEEK OUT

"Men of immature understanding begin an act without having an eye to what may happen in future." - Mahabharata

About six days later as we were walking near the river Ganga, we were met with a little surprise. Rohan was walking towards us away from a little hut. I saw a girl inside the hut with brown hair and long brown boots.

Rohan noticed us and stopped in his tracks.

"What are you doing here?" Satya asked, drawing her pocketknife.

Our weapons were all in my duffel bag, but I wasn't sure whether I should take them out or not. I mean, Rohan hadn't *done* anything yet.

Rohan didn't bother drawing his sword, "Visiting someone."

He gestured to the hut behind him, his eyebrows rising. Satya faltered when she saw the girl there who was staring at us curiously.

"Your choice," Rohan said, "But I would recommend waiting for the war. We wouldn't want anyone getting inspired, would we?"

He spoke coldly as if he wanted the girl to get inspired. Satya didn't move.

"What are we waiting for?" Sutasoma asked, "Just because some daredevil might get an earful from her father doesn't mean that we have to care."

Satya sighed, "We're not supposed to do anything before war. You know that."

She put the knife back in its tiny sheath and walked past Rohan in a huff.

Rohan nodded loftily, making Satya look as if she regretted her decision to walk away. She gestured for us to follow her. What was that? Who was that girl? Why didn't Satya do anything?

I know it's terrible of me to think this, but if we killed Rohan now, we wouldn't have to put up with any struggle at all. I stared at Rohan who stared back nonchalantly.

Once we had walked for a few feet I couldn't hold back my question, "Who was that girl?"

"Rohan's sister," Sutasoma replied, "I don't know *why* we did that, Satya. We could've finished him off and gotten the kingdom."

"One, that's not the right thing to do. It's against the code of righteousness to harm an enemy off the battlefield," Satya said, "Plus, you know how well Shishir and Nisata trained her. We may finish Rohan off, but she'll finish us off."

Who the hell were Nisata and Shishir?

Sutasoma didn't bother talking anymore. I didn't feel like asking any questions either. Seeing Rohan had brought back that memory of him in the airplane. The picture of Rohan's sneer when he called me *a queen* swam in my mind.

I was scared of becoming a queen. I knew full well that Rohan knew that too, but he also believed I couldn't do it. I should have believed that too, but *I* couldn't.

I suppose you're not cut out to be a leader after all.

It was like those multiple-choice questions where you get negative marking. You *know* you shouldn't guess the answer, but then…what if it was right?

The logical part of me knew the chances of me being a good ruler, though. I couldn't even command a group project at school. I only got an A+ on them because Riya took over.

I missed Riya…

I looked up at the sky, half expecting Riya and Emine to fall out of it. They were so much better at taking charge. Would it be wrong if I could give *them* the throne? Obviously, I'd need to come up with a good excuse, but that's *one* thing that I'm good at.

We hitched a ride on a bus using some of Satya's money. It was completely jammed in there as if all of India was going to the banks of Ganga.

By the time we got to the bus stop, it seemed like we'd spent all of eternity in the sweaty bus with the terrible driver. I was shocked we were still alive after *that* driving.

From the bus stop we stayed at a guest house in a small village near the river. The next morning, though, no one felt like walking to the next bus stop, and we didn't have internet to book a car. So, we decided to take a little break.

We went out to a huge tree a few meters from the guest house where we sat and spoke for a while.

"You want to see a little trick?" Akshara asked around noon, grinning.

She grabbed an apple out of her bag, pushed me towards the tree and placed the apple on my head.

"Woah," I said, seeing where this was going, "No, we're not doing this. I don't care if you're William Tell, but I'm no-"

"Oh, I'm not going to shoot. The only thing I inherited from Arjuna was music," Akshara smirked, handing a bow to Vedanth, "Vedanth will shoot."

Vedanth looked confused as if he'd read her lips wrong and pointed at himself questioningly. When Akshara nodded, he shrugged, stepped back, grabbed an arrow from his quiver and shot (way too casually. This was a terrible way to die). SMACK! It landed on the apple. Or so I assume because everyone else started cheering. *I* couldn't see it.

Relieved, I raised my hand to take the apple, but another arrow whizzed towards it splitting Vedanth's arrow in half.

I looked up in fear half-expecting Rohan to be standing there. Instead, there were two people. One of them, I knew.

"Riya!" I grinned, "What are you doing here?"

She really *had* fallen out of the sky!

"A few days after you left, I met this guy who told me I was this thing called... What was it?" Riya looked at the young man who arrived with her expectantly.

"KOMC," he said, then turned to the Pandavas' sons (PS for short), "Myna sent me to get her. I got to go to the USA before you, losers."

"Yeah, whatever," Riya nodded, "Anyway, turns out, I'm a kid of Arjuna and Princess Subhadra from the original Mahabharata."

"What?" I asked, frowning.

"Princess Subhadra," Riya prompted, "Krishna's sister."

Oh, right. I faintly remembered her from the show.

"Yeah. So, he took me to a drain that was a palace. There, I met this girl named Myna," Riya said, hardly stopping to take a breath, "And we got stuck in the palace for a night, because Myna wanted us to stay. Then she gave us directions that she got from this other guy and led us here."

"Yeah, Nisata told us you guys were here," the guy said as he walked over to the PS.

Again, with that dude. Who was Nisata?! I felt like I was missing out on something. Wasn't that guy Rohan's sister's friend? He was this guy's friend too?!

"That dude knows too much," Prathivindhya sighed, patting (more like slapping) the other guy's back.

"He apparently found out that you took a bus ride to this place from a friend of his," Riya laughed, "Can you believe this guy?"

"I heard that idiot Shrutakarma disappeared," the mystery guy said, "So I guess that makes me the only son of Arjuna here."

"No, you're not," Sahana rolled her eyes, gesturing to Vedanth who the mystery guy had probably not seen.

He turned to look at Sahana, "Nice to meet you, random person. I'm Abhimanyu."

That's when I started geeking out. It took every fiber in my body to restrain from squealing and jumping up and down. True that I didn't know much about the Mahabharata, but when we were watching that show about it, Abhimanyu became my favorite character.

He was the son of Arjuna and Subhadra (Lord Krishna's sister) too. In the original Mahabharata, he died in an unfair battle.

My mind quickly went back to right before we arrived at Panchalam when we were all sobbing over his death. Then I remembered that we were to *never* mention that.

"You're *Abhimanyu*?" I asked, trying to sound as normal as possible.

Riya nodded, excited.

Abhimanyu turned to me, smiling triumphantly "Well, *you* must be the to-be queen."

He bowed mockingly. I shrugged, deflating. Why did everyone know?

"Yeah, I guess," I murmured.

"So," Riya asked, "When are we reaching Magadha?"

"Why are we going to Magadha?" Abhimanyu asked.

I slapped my forehead, Amrita shook her head, and Riya made a tsk-tsk noise.

The PS took the time to be smart and explained everything to Abhimanyu. Then, we had to correct them and tell him the actual story where they did not punch the lights out of Asti, who had a million guards backing her up.

***

A few days later, we were passing by a large thicket of wood, and when we got out, we found ourselves in a large, orange, crowded city.

There were orange houses, orange carts, orange walls, orange doors, orange flags, and an orange palace.

Did I mention that there was a lot of orange?

"Oh, gods," Sahana said, averting her eyes, "The orange is blinding me."

I agreed. Who had decided to paint the whole city orange with the orange walls, the orange flags, and the orange fruits…

"That's a lot of flags," Amrita noted.

Satya pulled out her phone. Although it had no internet, she still had a map in her downloads.

"We have to go past the city," Satya said.

Sahana sighed, "If I turn blind after this remember that I won't be able to see the world because of you."

Satya scoffed, "Sure."

I stumbled, and quickly disguised it as a step, pretending to take initiative, "Let's go."

I walked down the steep hill towards the city wondering where we were, but it didn't take long for us to find out.

The first flag we saw had a monkey on it.

At once Satya, Abhimanyu and the PS screamed, "Ayodhya!"

They broke out in excited murmurs as the rest of us looked at each other in confusion.

"Ayodhya," Abhimanyu said, expectantly.

"Isn't that," I said, slowly, "the home of Lord Rama?"

"YES!" Satya said, excited, "I've never come here before!! I should have, but with all the training I never had time!"

"Oh! Lord Rama!" Shyamala realized, "From the Ramayana, right? What was the story again?"

Don't blame her. We'd been kept away from Hindu mythology for a while, but I had to know *who* Rama was *and* his story. All the temple trips we'd been to…

"Oh!" Sahana said, in realization after staring at the flag for a few more seconds, "Rama! Rama and Lakshmana, right?"

Abhimanyu nodded, "Yeah," he turned to Shyamala, "So there was a king called Dasharatha with three wives, but no sons. He really wanted an heir, so he conducted a yajna."

Amrita and Shyamala's jaw dropped, mine following.

Abhimanyu seemed confused by our surprise, "Right… so, Dasharatha got four sons, Rama, Lakshmana, Bharatha and Shatrughna- What is the big deal?!"

He spun around to where we were looking and let out a *Woah* sound.

Standing behind us was a huge figure who seemed to be half monkey and half man. The same one that was on the flag. At once Satya dropped to her knees in *pranam* and the rest of us followed in shock.

Even as I dropped to my knees, I couldn't help staring.

Hanuman was a close friend of Lord Rama. He was half man and half monkey and had stayed back on Earth instead of going to heaven to hear the story of Rama being told.

And that's what Abhimanyu was doing.

"No, don't stop," Hanuman smiled, "You're Krishna's nephew, aren't you? I met your uncle once. And your father."

Abhimanyu seemed at loss for words and stayed on his knees.

"Rise, children of the Pandavas," Hanuman told us, with a nod, "Welcome to Ayodhya."

I could imagine dramatic music blaring in the background. It didn't happen. Instead, Hanuman's voice resonated three times before he continued.

"Unfortunately, you will have to go past the city," Hanuman said, shaking his head, "It would be pleasant, but you are in a time constraint, and we are celebrating our king's birthday."

A few speakers started blaring a Rama bhajan, and there was a deafening cheer.

"So, the city is crowded," Hanuman said, "To speed along your journey, I am willing to take you on my back across the city."

"What?" I said, confused.

But he didn't hear me, and he started doubling in size, growing larger and larger. It was quite a sight to watch. The already tall monkey kept growing till he was taller than the Empire State Building.

"Oh," I gasped, figuring out the gist of what he'd said.

He knelt and held out his hands waiting for us to get on. Satya stepped on first followed by Abhimanyu leaving the rest of us with no choice but to do the same.

As I walked across the hand, I couldn't help but being impressed. I felt like I was walking on a wide road rather than what it actually was. As I walked towards Satya the hand rose and I fell.

As I got up, so did Hanuman and soon enough we were flying right across Ayodhya.

Hanuman chuckled, his voice quiet compared to his size, "Hold on tight."

I peeked down at the city where a man sat on an elephant that was being paraded down a long street. I couldn't help but laugh.

"Whoo!" I said, as the wind rippled through my hair.

Satya looked at me, grinning.

Sahana pumped her fist into the air, "Yass!!"

It was only as we were flying that I realized that Hanuman had gone past Ayodhya. As we passed a long river, I also realized that if Hanuman hadn't shown up, we would never have made it this far even after a week. Finally at the tip of another city that seemed twice as large as Ayodhya, Hanuman set us down.

"Good luck," he smiled, "I'm sorry I can't take you across your full journey."

Abhimanyu laughed as he stared at the city before us. "What do you mean? This is Magadha!"

Hanuman smiled knowingly, then turned to me.

"Princess Asti told me to give this to you," he said, handing me a small brass key, "It's something Rohan has been searching for, for a long time. In the center is the Syamantaka gem, a powerful gem that gives the holder endless money. If you keep it in the key, though, it won't. I trust you not to take it out, and to only keep it safe from Rohan. Do you understand?"

I nodded trying to process what he had said, taking the key from him.

He smiled and took off making the ground rumble beneath our feet.

"Let's do this," Satya smiled, and walked in.

SUBHADRAI

SHIPPED

"The man who suffers evil for his own misconduct should not attribute it to others." – Sanjaya, Mahabharata

I've tried to block the memory of the village of Magadha from my mind for a long time. The people in the streets looked at us as if we were about to whip them or kill them, and even if we were dressed in t-shirts and jeans, we still looked in a relatively better state than the people. I watched the citizens who seemed to be much older than us glance our way in fright. They looked at us as if they expected all of us to turn into blood-sucking vampires.

If only…

In about five minutes we were stopped by two guards at the gates of the looming palace.

One of them raised their hand gesturing for us to stop, "Ey, who are you?"

"I am the princess of-," I started, but Prathivindhya cut me off.

"We need to speak to the king. No arguments, take us to him," he snapped.

Someone didn't have enough patience for me to introduce myself.

The guard looked at him with a sneer, "Oh really? What kingdom are you from? You clearly don't know the rules around here."

And then, I had a genius idea.

"He's Rohan," I spat, "The prince of Hastinapura. He's literally about to take over half of India. You think you can stop him?"

The guard faltered and Prathivindhya, after a moment of shock, let out a sigh.

Then, I remembered that he couldn't lie, being Yudhisthira's son and the grandson of the god of righteousness.

"You," the guard said, staring at Prativindhya, "You're Rohan?"

"No," Sutasoma said, quickly before Prathivindhya could speak, "No, I'm Rohan, you fool! He's one of my servants. How dare you compare me to a filthy, no good, peasant!"

Prathivindhya stayed silent.

Maybe Sutasoma went a bit over the top, but the guards bought it.

"Yes, sir, we'll take you to the king. Along with these… filthy, no good, peasants?"

"Yes, of course," Sutasoma snapped, "I was expecting a chariot or at least a few snacks to welcome me, but I suppose this will have to do."

The guard turned to the other one and whispered an order to bring "Rohan" food.

Sutasoma turned and winked at us. I let out a sigh of relief. We were getting in.

I followed Sutasoma to the throne room where the king was talking to a lady in a parrot green sari.

It's Asti, Abhimanyu mouthed.

The king's head snapped towards us, 'Who are *you*?'

Sutasoma looked at me, questioningly.

"This is Rohan," the guard said, 'You know, the prince-'

"We're here for our brother," I said, walking in front of Sutasoma, my stomach churning.

If we were going to die, might as well let everyone say that I died talking to the scariest king in the world, bravely. I *hated* talking in front of people. It didn't help that this person had a huge sword and was seven feet above me.

But I decided that I needed to do this. I was going to rule a kingdom, so I was going to talk to this tyrant

The guard stared at me; his mouth open like a codfish.

"Shrutakarma," I said, menacingly.

At least, I hoped it was menacing. Once I was trying to scream at a kid for stealing my crayons and I ended up completely forgiving him and giving him a crayon as an apology for screaming at him.

So embarrassing.

The king didn't seem scared of me, not that I expected him to. He raised his eyebrows at the guard.

"Leave," he thundered.

The man scurried away as the other one walked in carrying a plate of laddus. Before the king could send him away, Sutasoma grabbed three and stuffed them in his mouth.

Once that guard had left the king cleared his throat.

He snorted, "Finally *somebody* comes looking for him. I thought no one cared. Although I expect that little light-travel block my daughter placed on you might have been the reason for that."

That's why we couldn't light-travel!

"You better let him go from your stupid prison right now," I threatened.

Woah. I was really good at this pretending-to-be-queen thing.

"Your brother isn't here," he said, picking up a grape from his golden bowl with a smug smile, "I have experienced many things. I am known all over India for my tolerance to pain. Jarasandha did *this*, Jarasandha did *that*. But I have *never* experienced a boy so annoying."

It took me a while to figure out who Jarasandha was, then remembered it was the king's name.

"What do you mean?" I asked, glancing at Satya, fear clouding my thoughts.

"I didn't like him, so I shipped him away," Jarasandha said, waving his hand carelessly.

My confidence faltered, "Shipped?"

"Yes. I sent him away. He *was* quite annoying if you know what I mean," Jarasandha said.

"SHIPPED?" Sutasoma roared, furiously, "WHERE?!"

The king, Jarasandha, nodded his head as Asti chuckled. I thought she was trying to help us!

"I had him sent across the sea. Far across the sea. To California. I own a resort there," Jarasandha sighed, and my jaw dropped, "The boy managed to escape my captivity and my sources tell me he's using my money and staying in my resort as a guest. I don't really mind, though. As long as he's out of my kingdom."

My jaw was literally on the floor as he continued, "Your brother is no longer my responsibility and never again will the prince of Hastinapura make me do something so painful ever again. Do not worry."

He looked tired as he waved us away.

I looked at the others, slightly relaxed to see that they were as shocked as I was. Jarasandha glanced at me.

I couldn't believe it.

After *all* this, Shrutakarma was staying in some resort in the exact place where I had JUST come from?!

I might have imagined this, but the king then locked his eyes with me.

"Subhadrai," He said, and I bit my tongue, "You will *never* be the ruler they all want you to be."

I glanced at the others. They seemed like they hadn't heard it. My nerves were getting better of me.

We left in silence, and the guards shot nasty glares at us as we left. Although I knew it wasn't my fault, I was left feeling almost guilty. I *could* be a good ruler, couldn't I?

***

I walked towards the village where we were going to rent horses, deep in thought. If I was ruling a kingdom, I'd have to speak to a bunch of important people. I'd have to, well, rule.

I couldn't do that.

I looked up at Satya. She'd been trained. She'd been told what to do when that huge golden crown was placed on her head.

I gulped. What if I messed up? What if they put the crown on my head and it slid off? What if I messed up so bad that the whole city died off? What if… what if Rohan won the war?

I got onto the horse that Satya had gotten me. My mom had put me in horse riding lessons three years ago, probably for a situation like this. It felt as if my whole life was already planned out. So, how did this story end?

The horse trotted past the sad village. I didn't pay attention to what the others were talking about. After a moment I looked down and realized my hands were shaking.

Was I *that* nervous? I looked around and saw that the others were shaking too.

"It's cold, isn't it?" Sahana asked, looking at me.

I felt a shiver run down my spine, as a strong gust of wind blew past me, "Yeah."

Our horses lurched forward, galloping towards a small garden and we clung onto the reins shivering as I turned to look behind me.

"WHAT IS GOING ON?" I screamed at Satya over the roar of the wind.

She looked at me, her eyes sparkling excitedly, "It's a summoning!"

I blinked, "What?"

She said something that sounded like *'a long saw is falling'*.

Ha. The wind was probably messing up my hearing. We came to a halt in front of a tree where a lady sat, staring at us expectantly. I slid off my horse staring at her in confusion.

Her dark eyes stared at us as her lips curled up with a gentle smile. Her black hair was tied in a braid that hung over a grape-colored sari. The main thing *I* noticed was that she had a lotus in one of her hands.

I'd never seen a lotus before.

Satya hastened to kneel before her and the rest of us followed. Once we'd risen, the lady opened her rose red lips.

"You have quite a journey in front of you," she said, "I hope you realize that you cannot take a plane all the way over the sea."

I frowned as Satya asked, "Um, why not?"

"Your enemy has every plane to California and back being monitored by his many spies," the lady sighed, "But I've decided to help you."

It was my turn to be stupid, "Why?"

The lady flashed me a soft smile, "I'm the wife of Dharma, Subhadrai. I always stay by him."

I frowned. The wife of Dharma? Satya let out a small gasp.

"Goddess Lakshmi?" she asked, after a moment of hesitation.

"I'm an incarnation of her," the lady said, "I'm Rukmini. The wife of Krishna."

My heart started beating faster. The wife of Krishna… the wife of Lord *Krishna!* I'd always imagined meeting normal celebrities like this singer or that actor, but this was so much better!

Rukmini turned her back towards us, "I'll provide you with a boat, which'll appear in the Bay of Bengal when you blow this. *Only* blow it when you reach the sea, though," she turned and handed Abhimanyu a whistle, with a wink "As for supplies, most of them will be on board the ship, including food and clothes. Here's a map," she handed Shrutasena a scroll, "although you won't need it. I suppose the boat will find its way across. The boy *is* in California, but to find him you'll need money. You, unfortunately, can't use Satya's, because your enemy has been tracking you through her phone, which you'll give to me. But, like I said, you still need money. For that, you came to the right goddess."

She flashed a sly smile. Lakshmi wasn't the goddess of wealth for nothing.

She gathered the coins that had fallen from her pot and put them in a sack and handed it to Vedanth in exchange for Satya's phone.

"Good luck on your journey to shore," Rukmini waved us off, and disappeared with a flash of light.

Abhimanyu turned to us, "I knew it was her the whole time. She's my aunt."

Riya rolled her eyes, "Quit the bragging, and let's go."

I got back onto the horse (with great difficulty. She was still shaken from Rukmini's calling.)

We started riding towards the Bay of Bengal which would obviously take a super long time, so Satya booked us three rooms at a hotel in Bihar.

"This place better have breakfast included," Sutasoma said as Satya gave the coins to the lady at the reception.

SUBHADRAI

NOSES ARE GOOD.

**"It is better for one to live on alms than to kill." –
Sanjaya, Mahabharata**

S o," I said, sitting down next to Satya in the hotel room, "We just met Rukmini."

She looked up at me, an eyebrow raised, "Oh, really? I didn't notice."

I let out a chuckle, "So, she's Krishna's wife?"

Satya nodded, "Yeah. Thank goodness. She was about to be Shishupala's wife."

I frowned, "How?"

Satya looked at me, "You don't know?"

I shook my head, "No, we weren't told those stories, remember? You were the only daughter of the Pandavas who grew up with mythology."

Satya nodded, "Right. So, basically, Rukmi, who's Rukmini's brother, was friends with the prince of Chedi, Shishupala."

Shyamala sat down next to me rubbing her hands, "Story time!"

"Rukmi promised Shishupala that he would give him his sister's hand in marriage," Satya continued as Amrita, Riya and Sahana stopped eating their veggie burgers to listen, "That's a high price to pay for friendship tax if you ask me. Anyway, Rukmini wasn't happy about it. *She* was intent on marrying Krishna."

"Exactly," Prathivindhya continued, trying to act smart (little did he know that he had a chopped-up piece of tomato hanging from his chin), "And so she sent a letter to Krishna telling him to come and take her away on the day of the marriage."

"That day, it seemed like everyone showed up except Krishna. Rukmini was worried that Krishna had decided not to show up," Sutasoma said, sitting down, taking Sahana's burger, "She was about to walk away from the crowd of chariots when Krishna arrived and took her into his chariot. Only as they were leaving did everyone else notice."

"After that, Krishna and Rukmini were being chased by an entire group of armies," Satanika said, "With only Balarama, Krishna's brother, and his army to defend them. But they got away and eventually Rukmi was the only one who followed. Krishna was about to kill Rukmi when Rukmini stopped him."

"They *are* siblings," Shrutasena pointed out.

"But Krishna shaved half the hair on his head off, along with half of his mustache which is a really insulting sign of a warrior's defeat," Abhimanyu said, "After that Krishna and Rukmini went back home where they got married and lived happily ever after."

I turned to Satya, "I thought *you* were telling the story."

She shrugged, "So did I."

***

"Oh gosh, these are heavy" Amrita said, dragging the currency Lakshmi had given us.

"What *is* this stuff?" I asked, picking up a coin from its bag.

"They don't look like rupees *or* pennies," Abhimanyu remarked.

"No lying, Sherlock." I muttered.

"When do we get to use the whistle," said Shrutasena, glancing at the red device hanging from Abhimanyu's neck.

"When we reach the shore," Satya said, patiently.

I frowned, looking at the map, "That means we can use it now. There's a river near us that empties at the ocean."

She shook her head, "Rukmini *clearly* mentioned that we have to summon the boat only when we reach the sea."

"Our first stop is Nalanda. Then we keep on going till we reach the shore," Akshara said, taking the map from me.

Vedanth signed something.

"It would take months to get there on foot. We need vehicles," Akshara said out loud, ignoring her brother.

"How about a train?" I suggested, pointing to a train station on the map, and Vedanth raised his eyebrows as if to say *I just signed that*.

Needless to say, everyone agreed to my amazing idea. Amrita and I lugged the money towards the station.

"I'll carry it myself," I insisted.

Amrita hesitantly agreed, but I didn't see what the big deal was. I carried the bag like it was a feather. I guess Bhima kids can do those things.

Once we reached the train station, Satya walked over to a man behind the counter.

"Is there a train that goes to the shore of the Bay of Bengal?" She inquired, looking at the table that seemed to be as ancient as the man sitting behind it.

"Maybe. Do you have money?" The man asked.

I took out a handful of the strange coins. The man's eyes widened.

"You *are* mid-heroes, aren't you?" The man asked.

"Er…. yes… I mean, no. We're KOMC," I said.

The man's eyes widened and he nodded taking the money, "Normally, I wouldn't let you on my train unless you had a ticket, but since you *are* KOMC…"

Satya told us later that mid-heroes are kids of mythological people and normal people. Those children are half-hero, half-normal, so mid-hero.

"We have a train coming in at around 5:00," the man said, "I'll give you tickets now, but next time you do this, be sure to prebook. We don't generally encourage this sort of behavior."

"Stop being a mom and give it," Abhimanyu snapped.

Sahana raised her eyebrows at him, "Show him some respect. He's helping us!"

Abhimanyu rolled his eyes, "I can't believe you're trusting this dude. He could be that guy from that weird soda ad!"

"Isn't that guy animated?" Sutasoma asked.

Abhimanyu shrugged, "Beats me. How would I know?"

I shook my head as Satya turned back to the man, "But, seriously, could you please give us the tickets."

The man frowned at us, "I haven't worked the ticket machine in *years*. Wait."

He pressed a few more buttons and after a while one single ticket emerged.

"It'll be midnight before we get those tickets," I groaned.

Amrita looked at the ticket machine, "Um. Can you turn up the speed dial?"

"It's broken," The man said.

"You never tried it," Amrita protested.

"I know it's broken," the man sighed.

"I don't think so. You said you haven't worked it in years," Amrita pointed out.

"Just because no one used it doesn't mean that it was fixed," the man retorted.

Amrita groaned, "Why is nobody else thinking that this is suspicious? He could be a Kaurava spy slowing us down while Rohan takes his time to show up and kill us!"

The man looked up, "What happened to your patience. Did God skip that part for you?"

"Wait," Satya said, "Amrita's right. You didn't ask for details or anything. How would you book us a ticket?"

The man bit his lip as Amrita reached out for the machine he was working on. She wiped some dust off it.

"*Instadial*," I read off the board, "Seriously? This thing is from the stone ages you should seriously upgrade. I mean-"

"YOU'VE CALLED ROHAN!" Amrita screamed, drawing her sword.

There came a tutting from behind us.

We whipped around expecting to see Rohan's slimy face but instead we got...

"Surpanakha!" Satya threw her hands up in the air, obviously annoyed by the lady without a nose who stood before us, "Seriously? Come on! Does Rohan have *no* bounds? SURPANAKHA?!"

"You know, lately, people have been respecting me," Surpanakha said, "They've been calling me mistreated, misunderstood-"

"A mistake," Abhimanyu growled, "because *people* seem to also have forgotten the fact that you tried to *kill* Sita!"

"Um, excuse me?" Shyamala asked, "What's going on?"

"Oh right, you don't know the Ramayana," Satya sighed. "So basically-"

"No, I remember now. I'd just forgotten the beginning," Shyamala said, "There was a prince named Rama. He was an incarnation (avatar) of Vishnu. He, his wife, and his brother were exiled to the forest because his stepmother didn't want him to be king. During his stay in the woods, this lady-"

"Me," said the lady, "Surpanakha."

"She showed up. She was actually a demon, but she changed her form to look like a human," Shyamala continued, "She asked Rama to marry him, but Rama rejected her because he promised Sita that she would be his only wife. Then Surpanakha went and asked Lakshmana to marry her, but Lakshmana said that marrying her would distract him from his responsibility of protecting Rama, so he cut off Surpanakha nose."

"Er, no," Satya said, "Close, except-"

"Surpanakha was angry that both Rama and Lakshmana rejected her, that she tried to kill Sita," Abhimanyu said, matter-of-factly, "And *then* Lakshmana cut off her nose."

Surpanakha nodded sadly, "Yes, I no longer have a nose, because of Lakshmana's rage."

"*Your* rage," I pointed out, thoughtfully, "You tried to kill Sita."

"Yes, I did, but that was in my past life," Surpanakha said, "I'm good now."

"You're working for Rohan," Prativindhya pointed out.

"Yes, and?" Surpanakha rolled her eyes, "I don't even get why you guys are *fighting* him. You give him Hastinapura, you get Indraprastha."

"Last I checked, he wanted *both*," Satanika thought out loud.

"Oh, yeah, he does," Surpanakha said, "I forgot about that. Well, you should give it to him. Oldest gets it, right?"

"Still the oldest," Satya raised her eyebrows.

"Wait," said the train ticket man, "Wait, Satya's the oldest?"

Surpanakha nodded, "Yeah, but Rohan's way better at ruling."

"How would you *possibly* know that?" Sahana asked, "You haven't seen him rule."

"Yes, I have," Surpanakha said, "He's literally my boss."

The train man nodded as if to say, *Point*.

"Alright, but the first born should be the first to rule," Satya snapped, "Subhadrai is older than Rohan, so it's only fair that *Subhadrai* becomes queen."

"If a backup like Subhadrai can become a ruler, Rohan can too," The train man decided, "Plus, Subhadrai hasn't even been trained. What does she know of ruling?"

"Subhadrai's a natural," Satya said, fiercely "And, Rohan doesn't want any good for the kingdom. He wants to impress his *dad* who wants to prove that-"

"He's changed," Surpanakha finished, "And he has."

Shyamala slowly drew her sword making sure nobody noticed. I did. I was trying to focus on everything except the conversation about me.

"No, he hasn't!" Satya said, 'Thanks to him, here we are, in war, again.'

Surpanakha sighed, "Listen, Rohan's not as bad as you think. He's trying to do what his dad wants him to do, which isn't going great, but it's all he *can* do, alright?"

"Ugh, what are you doing here?" Shyamala asked, cutting the conversation.

"I'm here to stop you from finding your brother," Surpanakha said.

"Oh, okay," she nodded, "That sounds good enough."

Shyamala lunged her sword towards her, but before reaching her gut, Surpanakha disappeared.

"Shyamala!" Satya cried.

"Heartless," Sutasoma said, with his eyebrows raised.

"I was getting tired," Shyamala shrugged, "We'll be riding on that train, tickets or no tickets."

ROHAN

A NAP IN THE DUMPSTER

"A person should never do that to others, which he does not like to be done to him by others." – Bhishma, Mahabharata

"ROHAN! DINNER!"

I jolted awake and checked the time. 7:10. I rolled out of bed and scrambled into the bathroom, trying to make myself look as least exhausted as possible.

Shakuni had *really* messed me up.

"COMING!" I called, as I ran down the stairs of the kingdom of Chedi.

Previously, we'd been staying at my aunt's palace, the Sindhu kingdom. But as much as my father likes his sister, her husband is really annoying. So, we made up some stupid excuse and went to my dad's best friend's kingdom, Chedi.

Of course, the king, Shishupala, is not as evil as he was in the original epic anymore.

In the original Mahabharata, he was given a hundred pardons from Lord Krishna, and if he insulted Krishna a hundred times, he'd be killed.

He crossed the line in less than an hour.

Now, he's kind of nice to be around. My only problem is his son, Anish.

"Watch where you're going," Anish scowled, as he bumped into me on purpose, "Where've you been all day? It looks like you've been taking a nap in the dumpster."

I ignored him and ran into the dining room, where Anish's grandmother and my mother were waiting.

"Rohan, I'm really worried about you," Bhanumati said, as she stroked my hair when I entered, "You haven't been sleeping well. Do you miss your sister? I can arrange another visit if you'd like."

"No, it's okay," I said, stuffing a dosa into my mouth.

"What did she say last time you saw her?" Anish's grandmother asked, curiously.

"Nothing much," I lied.

She'd told me that she was sick of the Kaurava family and the first chance she got, she was going to leave our father.

Not really worth the mention.

"Rohan, your father's coming home from the meeting tomorrow," Bhanumati said, "You might want to fix your sleep schedule by then."

"Yeah, yeah," I said, stuffing a dosa in my mouth, taking two in my hand, "Love you. Bye."

I ran up and tripped against a little toy car Anish had probably left on the stairwell. I cursed under my breath as I got up and headed towards my room.

I sank into bed with a sigh, eating another dosa.

What was wrong with me?!

I looked at the picture of the key that I'd found in the library at Sindhu.

Groaning, I got up and picked the picture up. I glanced at it one last time before I dropped it into the trash can.

I picked my sword up and decided to practice using it for a while. I'd been cooped up for days. I walked over to the garden where I heard voices.

"Ambika!"

"I never expected she would do that."

"It can't be true."

I stopped stabbing the dummy to listen.

"He went to check on her an hour ago," Bhanumati said, in hushed tones, "She wasn't there,"

"But I thought you left Surpanakha to guard her."

I hit my forehead. No! I'd sent Surpanakha to the train station to take care of the Pandavas' kids yesterday! I felt like stabbing myself. I threw the sword at the training dummy, and it landed somewhere near the cricket field, five meters away.

Ignoring what I'd heard, I spent the rest of the day trying to stab the dummy in frustration. If Ambika really had chosen to "leave her father", we were dead.

In an hour or so, there was a flash of light and Surpanakha appeared, "Your majesty, she escaped!"

"I know," I said, "Great job. Do you want a prize?"

"Sir, the PD are going to the shore of the Bay of Bengal. They were given a conch by Lakshmi," she said, "Remember the conch that Shishupala told you about?"

I did. He'd told me about a small white conch that Rukmini's brother owned that could summon a boat to the nearest ocean.

"Sir, you should send *her* to the boat," Surpanakha said.

It took me a second to process who she was talking about.

I grinned, with an appreciating nod. It was about time my best spy was used. I told her to send *her*.

The girls were in for *quite* a surprise.

That's when my cousin, Advaith ran into the garden with a smile on his face.

SUBHADRAI

PLEASE TELL ME I'M DREAMING

"Men lose good judgment in things which concern their interest." – Dhritarastra, Mahabharata

It took a while to find another train station. They should really put train stations near each other. It's pretty annoying. Once we got off the train we'd found, we had to walk for another hour to get to the shore. Once we were there, Abhimanyu didn't waste a beat before blowing the whistle.

I stared at the water expecting a boat to appear.

"You didn't blow it right," Sahana decided, "Give it to me."

"Who said *you* were a whistleblowing expert?" Amrita's brows burrowed, "I can play the flute."

"You cann*ot*!" I argued.

"I didn't blow it wrong!" Abhimanyu said, firmly, "The boat is probably far away."

"I think that maybe the eldest should blow it," Satya speculated.

"The eldest boy," Prativindhya corrected.

"Still me, in both cases" Abhimanyu reminded him, his eyebrows raised.

"Oh right, *you*," Prativindhya deflated.

"How about we take turns," Sahana decided, "I call going first."

Sahana grabbed the whistle from Abhimanyu, but he pulled it back. Amrita tried to pull it from him and in all the commotion the whistle fell. I think that they accidentally pressed a hidden button and a glow of light swirled around the whistle and in its place a small white conch appeared.

"I'll do this," I said, picking up the conch taking advantage of everyone's shock.

I held the end to my lips and blew, but all that came out was the sound of a cat dying. Oof.

"I've been trained to do this," Abhimanyu smirked, "Give it to me."

"If you've been trained to do it, then train me," I said, pulling the conch away sharply.

Abhimanyu demonstrated holding a conch and blowing. I imitated it. It sounded like a cat dying less painfully.

"You're a bad teacher," I deduced.

"Blow more forcefully," Prathivindhya advised, "And pucker your lips."

"Ew," I said, "Abhimanyu will blow it."

I handed it to him, and he blew it. A long resonant sound vibrated throughout the area and *then* a ship came speeding towards us, stopping so quickly, I thought it was going to topple over.

I drew in a breath.

It was *huge*. It'd take a few *years* to look through the whole ship. I hoped that it was faster than it looked, because I wasn't sitting on the sea for a few months to find *Shrutakarma*.

"Alright," I said, once we were all on board, "Who works this thing?"

"I work it," said a voice behind us, "I'm your guide, Saanvi."

Behind us stood a girl in a long dress and *Captain Hook* hat that didn't suit her at all. Not everyone can pull that look off successfully.

"Did Rukmini send you?" Satya asked, squinting at the newcomer.

"Uh, yeah," Saanvi agreed, "Duh."

"How'd you get onto the boat?" Shrutasena asked, his voice glazed with suspicion.

"I climbed on," Saanvi said, "How stupid are you?"

"When?" Abhimanyu questioned.

"After you guys," Saanvi rolled her eyes, "No one told me it would be so hard to convince you guys that I'm *not* a Kaurava lieutenant. RUKMINI sent me!"

I looked at Satya who shrugged.

"Alright, whatever," she said, "Mind showing us around, then?"

"Er, no," Saanvi said, "Of *course* I can show you around."

She put her hand up, the lion ring on her hand glinting, "This is the wheel."

"Oh, *really?*" Sahana asked, crossing her arms, "I *never* knew!"

She turned to us and mouthed, *Are we really trusting her?*

Saanvi turned to Sahana, annoyed, "*This* is the deck."

Sahana glanced at the floor and mimicked looking interested, "Go on!"

Saanvi walked towards a little building, her dark, familiar boots clanking on the wooden floor.

I turned to Satya, "I don't trust her. Nobody wears a hat like that and isn't evil."

Saanvi came back out.

"Why aren't you following? You're supposed to *follow*," she said, shaking her head, "I can't be the guide if you stay up there."

We clambered down the steps that ended at a large hallway with fourteen bedrooms.

Seeing that we were more interested in our rooms than her tour, Saanvi hurriedly sent us to our rooms and promised that she would continue the next day.

During breakfast (which appeared in the morning out of thin air. Goddesses are the best), we discussed our route. Saanvi must have lit some scented candles because the place smelled wonderful.

"If only Indian mythology had a sea monster that would help us speed up," Abhimanyu sighed.

"Does it?" I asked, my eyes gleaming in excitement.

"Um, probably," Satya said, "But I don't think-"

The boat lurched forward, and in a moment, Saanvi came into the room carrying a half-eaten croissant, "Uh, *you* guys are the heroes. This is *your* job."

I followed Satya to the deck with Sahana trailing behind me. There, in the sea before us, was a fishing boat with a lady seated inside. As we neared her, the fragrance grew and I realized that she'd been emitting it the whole time, not some stupid candle.

"Who *is* she?" I asked, squinting at her.

My mind raced trying to think of a visual match. I stared at the boat. In it was a fishing net and a crown of flowers. I bit my tongue. A fisherwoman...

"No way, I thought she would have died again," Satya said.

A ladder dropped and Satya climbed down to the boat in which the lady was standing. In an instant, Satya was thrown back onto the deck in a large fishing net.

"She wants Subhadrai," Satya winced, looking at me.

What? Why would she want me?

I braced myself to be thrown back onto the deck too and climbed down the ladder.

Who was this lady?

My feet landed on the deck of the boat where the lady was waiting.

"Finally," she smiled, "You're the daughter of Bhima!"

I nodded, acting confident (emphasis on 'acting'), "Um, yeah, I noticed."

"You know, the others are so… ignorant. They won't notice," the lady said, throwing her hands in the air, "But I'm sure you, the future *queen*, will be quick to catch on."

Her simple off-white sari rustled as a gust of wind pushed the light boat further from our large one.

"Subhadrai, you *must* listen to me," the lady insisted, "You are not safe."

"Yeah, I know *that* too," I said, my confidence growing, "There's this war coming up. I don't know if you-"

"Right now," the lady said, frowning, "I'm serious."

"Right," I nodded, "Okay. Um, who are you?"

"Your great-great-grandmother," the lady said, "I'm Satyavati."

I stared at her, "I'm sorry, I've never heard of you."

"How far do you know your ancestry line?" Satyavati asked, frowning.

"Um," I tried to recall how far I knew my family went, "From Dhritarashtra."

Satyavati shook her head in disappointment, "Well, let me start with King Shantanu. Listen carefully, Daughter of Bhima. This is your test."

And she started speaking.

"There once was a king named Shantanu," Satyavati said, "He was fond of hunting and one day as he was hunting, he encountered a beautiful lady near the river Ganga. He fell for her at once and the lady agreed to marry him on one condition. He could never question her. At all."

"And he agreed?" I asked, bemused.

"He did," Satyavati scowled, "He did not know who the lady was, but they got married. Eventually, they had a child. Shantanu was elated, but the lady cast the child away into the sea. The poor king could do nothing about it. This happened seven times, but on the eighth child, the king couldn't take it anymore."

"Oof," I winced, "He questioned her."

"Oof indeed," Satyavati agreed, "The lady left him, took the child with her and Shantanu was left alone. Until, one day, he saw a boy near the banks of the river Ganga and he asked the boy who his parents were. You can imagine how shocked he was when he realized that the child was his son, and his mother was..."

She waited for me to guess. I wrung my hands.

A boy. Shantanu. Hunting. The river.

"Ganga!" I exclaimed, "The river Ganga's goddess."

Every river has a goddess, and Ganga was one of the major ones.

"Wonderful," she clapped, "Ganga sent her son named Devavrata to Shantanu and the king trained his son to become king. But then one day, the king was hunting again, and he saw another lady."

"Not *again*," I groaned.

Satyavati nodded, "Again, he fell in love with her. This lady was a fisherwoman. She had a strong, sweet fragrance."

Again, my mind started racing.

Fragrance. Fisherwoman. Strong.

"You," I gasped.

The story was starting to make sense.

"Precisely," Satyavati nodded, "but my father wouldn't allow me to leave. He gave Shantanu a condition that stated that he could only marry me as long as only my children would rule the kingdom. If that condition was fulfilled, he could marry me."

"Poor king," I sighed, "Everyone's being so rude to him!"

Satyavati nodded, pitifully, "Anyway, the king returned home, distraught, because Devavrata was supposed to be king. Devavrata noticed something was wrong with his father and so he went to the forest where the fisherwoman was. Upon hearing the condition that my father had given Shantanu, Devavrata took an oath to never become king and to never marry so he wouldn't have sons who would take over the kingdom."

"Woah," I muttered, "Hardcore."

Satyavati sighed, "Of course. It was necessary, though. It was *me* at stake. He was then named Bhishma, because of the oath he'd taken. The name meant 'The Terrible One'."

I gasped. Talk about a plot twist. It was like a country song where they talk for a long time about someone and then say, *it's him, that guy you know!*

"I got married to Shantanu and had two sons. They married two princesses, but my sons died leaving their wives childless. That would mean the end of our dynasty, but I have my ways…," Satyavati said.

"I know it from here," I said, "A sage named Veda Vyasa showed up. He blessed the princesses, and they gave birth to Pandu and Dhritarashtra. The rest is history."

Satyavati looked as if she was about to launch into more of the story, but luckily, Satya saved me.

"HEY," Satya called, "WE HAVE A DEADLINE, SO IT WOULD BE GREAT IF YOU COULD FINISH THIS SWEET CONVERSATION QUICKLY!"

Satyavati looked at me, "Subhadrai, you've passed my test."

And with that, she leaned in and started whispering.

SUBHADRAI

BOAT ON FIRE

In this world, the relationship between the virtuous is more important than a relationship resulting from birth
– Bhishma, Mahabharata

I returned to the deck with Saanvi waiting in front of me.

"Well?" Saanvi asked, impatiently.

"None of your business," I snapped, rolling my eyes, "Come on, guys, let's go down. I'm starving."

I walked towards our rooms and gestured for the others to follow, my eyebrows raised, "Coming?"

"That's our cousin," Abhimanyu sighed, "The queen of patience."

They followed me to Satya's room.

"You should've been nice to her," Satya snapped, "She's helping us!"

"You don't get it," I argued, "She's from the Kauravas!"

Satya groaned, "We've gone over this a million times. She isn't!"

"Oh?" I said in frustration, "Have you noticed her boots? Rohan's sister was wearing them when we saw her in the woods. And the lion ring on her hand? I can't believe we didn't notice it before! It's the symbol of the Kauravas!"

They stared at me deep in thought.

"No way," Amrita muttered, "How do we know if she's taking us to the right palace?"

"She wasn't," I muttered, "That's why Satyavati (that's who I was talking to by the way) created a portal with goddess Ganga's help. We've been transported. We're arriving at the Golden Gate bridge in," I checked my watch, "zero seconds."

There was a scream of anger from the deck and I smirked, "That's our Kaurava friend realizing that we're *way* smarter than her."

There was a *thunk* on the deck and another scream from Saanvi. Of terror.

"And *that* is our cue to go up," I muttered.

We didn't hesitate for a second. I ran up to the deck where Saanvi was pinned to the mast by a bunch of arrows. In front of her, was a girl, probably eleven years old, staring at us with expectancy. She looked familiar…

Then, to prove that she could handle Saanvi too, Sahana drew an arrow and nearly shot Saanvi. *She* says nearly.

Don't listen to what Satya says about the arrow landing in the water.

It started to drizzle, and the rain gradually grew into a downpour.

"Sorry," the girl said, "Did *you* want to freak her out? I got carried away."

I noticed the boots that she was wearing, and gasped. It was Rohan's sister.

Satya stared at her, "Ambika, if your father finds out that you're-"

"It doesn't matter," the girl, Ambika, waved her hand in a careless manner, "I want to join *you* guys."

Prathivindhya snorted.

Sutasoma slapped his forehead.

"I mean it!" Ambika said, her eyes gleaming, "I know a *lot* of things about the Kaurava army. I could pretend to be on both sides!"

"YOU CAN'T KEEP ME QUIET!" Saanvi screamed from the mast.

"Um, yes I can," Ambika turned to Saanvi, "I'm the princess. That's my *job*."

Saanvi frowned, "Not-"

"Shut up, Saanvi," Ambika sighed, and Saanvi did, "*As I was saying*, I'm very useful. Plus, Satya, I heard you weren't in charge of Indraprastha anymore."

Ambika turned to me with a smile that said, *I'm so much better than you.*

My stomach churned. I couldn't refuse the offer, could I? As long as we kept watch on her at all times, then I guess it would be fine. I *had* to stop Rohan from ruling.

Something told me that if I didn't accept this offer, I would never get the kingdom that belonged to *me*. But if I did, I would disappoint everyone who was expecting me to tell the kid to get lost.

Luckily, I didn't need to answer because lightning struck the wooden boat starting a fire. Saanvi screeched.

"LEMME OUT! LEMME OUT!" she hollered, "WHAT ARE YOU DOING?! QUIT WASTING TIME!"

"I'm only leaving this boat when queenie here answers me," Ambika said, flashing her eyes at me. I was too panicked to think straight. I wasn't going out like this!

"Uh yeah, sure, you can join us. But we'll have to always keep watch on you," I nodded, nervously, as the fire spread towards us. Ambika nodded, satisfied.

"So, are you going to burn along with this ship, or...?" she raised her eyebrows at us.

We shook our heads quickly. As I was about to jump out, a thought struck me, and I ran to a small closet near the wheel and took the key Hanuman gave me out of the drawer and clenched it tightly.

"Come on," I said nervously and jumped off the ship into the cold water.

We swam to the shore to see Ambika there waiting for us with Saanvi.

"You… you can travel light?" I asked, incredulously.

"Uh, yeah," she shrugged.

She helped me up from the water and climbed the cliff up the street where I stuffed the key into my pocket quickly hiding it from Ambika.

"So..." Satya said, looking at Ambika "Why are you joining our side?"

"I'm not joining your side," Ambika said, laughing, "I *already* joined! You heard Subhadrai."

"Right," Satya said, not looking as disappointed as I expected her to be, "Why've you already joined the Pandavas?"

"Well," Ambika said, walking down the sidewalk, "It started when I put sour cream in my dad's samosa."

"Oof," Sutasoma muttered, "Please don't tell Shrutakarma that. We don't need him getting any ideas."

"Yeah, that didn't go too well. Then, my dad found out I was learning how to swordfight," Ambika sighed, "And he got scared that I might challenge Rohan, so he sent me to a tiny hut in the middle of nowhere"

"Well, if it was you who pinned Saanvi to the wall, that was good," Prathivindhya said.

Abhimanyu looked at him with an expression that said '*You're complimenting her?*'

"I can't lie," Prathivindhya said, innocently.

"Yeah, well I learnt how to do that that by myself," Ambika said, proudly, "And Nisata helped me with some."

"No way," Sutasoma groaned, "I'm so sick of that dude."

Again, with Nisata…Who *was* he?

"Yeah, I know right," Ambika shook her head, "Anyways, my dad made a mistake. I hate him now, though I don't really hate Rohan. But I do want him to see that a queen can rule too. I want Subhadrai to win!"

I smiled, but (I could have been imagining it) I thought I heard sarcasm in her voice.

"Well now that we've gotten this sorted out, let's find that miserable boy and get his stupid butt out of California," Ambika grinned.

She tried to shake my hand, but she let go of Saanvi who light-traveled away in less than a second.

Ambika cursed, and I glanced at Satya in worry.

"It's okay, she can't do anything," Satya said, "We have Ambika."

***

"Is this it?" I asked, looking at the huge hotel in front of us.

We'd taken a cab to the five-star hotels near the bay. This was our fifth try, but it was the last one, so Shrutakarma *had* to be here.

We walked into the reception, and I walked to the counter.

"Excuse me, do you have a guest named Shrutakarma?" I asked politely.

It was crazy that this actually worked.

"I'm sorry, ma'am," the receptionist said, looking up at me, "We can't give you that information unless-"

"We're family," I said, "And his parents are looking for him everywhere, and someone told us he might be staying here."

The receptionist stared at me uncertainly, "Alright, I'll call him down."

He picked up the phone and whispered something. The person on the other end replied.

"He's in the spa, ma'am," the receptionist told me, "He'll be down in five minutes."

I nodded, "Thank you so much, sir."

I turned around and walked towards the group, "He's in the spa."

Sahana gritted her teeth as Riya sighed with exasperation. Vedanth signed something that didn't look too nice.

"Why does he have to be *our* brother," Sutasoma sighed, "He could have done this to anyone else!"

"Hey guys," said a voice behind us.

There stood Shrutakarma in a Hawaiian t-shirt, shorts, and slippers, "Guys, this hotel is amazing! It hardly costs anything!"

"Says the rich prince with the palace," Sahana murmured.

"The *spa*," Shrutakarma shook his head in wonder, "First class, trust me."

"Yeah, okay, rich kid," I muttered, "Now let's get out of this place so we can *talk*."

He followed us to the exit and once we got out, Sahana slapped him across the face, "We had to go halfway around the world to find you!"

"Your fault," Shrutakarma shrugged, "I was fine. I booked plane tickets and everything."

"Plane tickets?" I asked, "You can light-travel!"

"I wanted to try planes. They sound cool," Shrutakarma told me, a glint in his eye.

"Well, I hope we can light-travel now, at least," I sighed, "We'll leave you here so you can enjoy your plane ride."

Sahana shook her head, "I'm *never* helping you again. Sons of heroes end up being idiots with too much money."

"Um, I don't really know where we're going now," Ambika piped up, "So, I need to hold someone's hand if you're light-traveling."

"Myna sent the address for the new camp yesterday in our chat," Shrutakarma said, "Let me go get it."

HE KNEW THE ADDRESS?! I couldn't believe it...

Once he came back with a slip of paper, with the address on it, his face turned serious, "If you couldn't light-travel, it would've taken you a long time to come here."

"Yes, genius," I said, rolling my eyes.

"But that means you've helped Rohan," Shrutakarma pointed out, "You gave him a week or more than that to recruit more armies for war. Armies that *you* could've gotten if you didn't come looking for me."

I stared at him. Was the idiot actually making a point? I turned to Satya who'd turned pale.

"Ambika, how many kingdoms has Rohan recruited?" the daughter of Yudhishthira asked.

"When I left, five," Ambika said.

I was pretty sure that we had none.

"We'll worry about this later," Satya decided, closing her eyes in what seemed like disappointment, "We have to get back to camp *now*."

Shrutakarma waved us goodbye, and we light-traveled to the camp, straight into battle. To make matters worse, I threw up over the floor.

SUBHADRAI

THE SYAMANTAKA GEM

"War causes destruction to all, it is sinful, it creates cell, it gives the same result in victory and defeat alike," – Sanjaya, Mahabharata

Although there was total pandemonium, I focused on Rohan. I sprinted up the hill to where Rohan was standing. When I'd gotten up to him, the key that Hanuman had given me decided to fall out of my pocket.

"The Syamantaka Gem!" Rohan muttered, a crazed look in his eye, "You had it the whole time!"

He bent down to pick it up, but I got it before him.

"You want the key, you got to get through me," I said, then thought *Hey, That rhymes!*

"Fine," Rohan snarled, and he unsheathed his sword.

I did the same.

He raised his weapon and I slipped under him, grabbing the key. It was a move I'd learnt with Satya, who was at least a foot taller than me. Thank *goodness* Rohan was too. I stuffed the key back into my pocket.

He tackled me, and I pushed him off. Ugh, the key had fallen out again. Pockets should have their own security guards. Rohan and I fell to our knees at the same time and searched for the key frantically. Unfortunately, both of us spotted it at the same time too.

I lunged towards it, but Rohan pushed me back and grabbed it.

"Give. it. BACK!" I screamed and tackled him. We pushed and kicked each other, and the key moved from hand to hand.

"WHY DO YOU NEED IT?" I shouted, grabbing the key from the grass.

"It gives the owner power. Duh," Rohan said, rolling his eyes.

I blinked. Really? I thought it just gave money.

"Why do you want it?" Rohan asked, grabbing the key, and trying to run.

"BECAUSE *YOU* WANT IT," I protested without thinking, tripping him, and grabbing the key.

"ATTACK!" came a voice behind me, "YOU SHALL PERISH!"

Rohan and I stared at the figure at the same time, still fighting for the key.

The ground rumbled and a few monkeys wearing diapers lunged at Rohan.

I smiled at the looming figure before us commanding the smaller monkeys.

Lord Hanuman had helped us once more.

A monkey bit Rohan's cousin, Advaith, who yelped in pain and let go of Vijay whom he was holding captive.

"You kids fall into trouble quite easily," Hanuman said.

I glared at Rohan who was still getting the diaper monkey off. There was chaos everywhere. The Kauravas were still doing pretty well for the number of KOMC against them. I lashed my sword at Rohan who glared at the key in my hand.

"I can win without it," He smirked, and he raced down the hill, "I've got one last thing to do."

There was ringing silence for two beats and then I heard Satya scream. I ran towards the sound and there, lying on the floor was Myna's body with Rohan standing over it, wiping the blood off his sword on her purple t-shirt.

I gasped, my knees threatening to give away.
No.

"Myna," Satya said, slowly walking towards Myna, her hands trembling.

She knelt down as Myna gasped, struggling for breath.

"Come on, Myna," Satya said, holding back tears, "Say something."

She looked around for help, but no one was paying attention. Everyone was fighting their own fight. Kauravas were appearing by the second, and no one bothered to glance at us.

Myna let out another gasp, clutching at the grass beneath her, but still, she said nothing.

Rohan shook his head as if he was awakening from a dream and stared at Myna. He made a face that looked like shock, but the blood on his sword…it belonged to Myna.

Satya then looked up, and let out a guttural scream, lunging herself towards Rohan. Myna lay behind her in the grass, now motionless.

I staggered backwards, my eyes shut.

"You *traitor*!" Satya howled, trying to choke Rohan, who looked just as shocked as her.

He clutched at Satya's hands, but she didn't look like she was letting him go without killing him, and the son of Duryodhana looked as if he was about to pass out from shock.

He then looked at me. His face hardening with pure hatred, and he pushed Satya away with what seemed like no effort.

"I only came to ask for help," he said, "Myna attacked first."

Satya, who was about to draw her dagger stopped midway, "What?"

Rohan stepped away from Satya, sheathing his sword, with a cruel smirk.

"No," Satya shook her head, "She wouldn't…It's not …That's not right.".

"Too bad," Rohan said, with a scowl, "Not everyone is as righteous as you'd want them to be."

Satya looked at Rohan as if he was from another world, and then back at Myna's body which lay as still as stone.

She fell to her knees, and Rohan hollered, "Fall back!"

One by one the Kauravas disappeared until only Rohan seemed to be left.

He glanced at Myna one more time, and he too went with the light.

"She attacked first," came a voice behind me.

I whirled around in fright, grappling for my sword which was tied at my hip.

Advaith looked at Myna, his eyes not meeting mine, "But Rohan captured her brother."

There was one more blinding flash of light, and I felt a shiver run down my spine.

Satya was staring at empty ground, as still as Myna. I drew in a shaky breath as the other PD came up to me along with Vijay.

Rohan had captured *him* making Myna attack.

It was his fault.

It was Rohan's fault.

It was *my* fault.

Rohan only killed her because I didn't give him the stupid key. I pulled it out of my pocket and dropped it onto the floor.

He could have it for all I cared. It wouldn't change a thing, because I was still going to sit on that throne in the end.

No.

Matter.

What.

***

Two weeks passed in what felt like complete silence. Hardly anyone ever spoke, until Satya came up to our camp on Monday.

"Bhishma's calling me for a meeting," she said, her voice hoarse, "You guys stay here, alright? No one should leave."

I glanced at Amrita who didn't look back. A meeting? For what?"

It didn't take me long to find out. Satya came back moments later, and called me out to the field, but still wouldn't meet my eye.

"He said that you and Rohan should remain in your camps, and not engage in war, until he comes up with a decision on how to choose the rulers."

"Satya."

Her head jerked up and her eyes met mine.

"I'll win. Don't worry."

PART TWO

THE ARMIES

SUBHADRAI

OHMYGODSOHMYGODS!!

"He that is wise and patient performs life's journey in peace." – Vidura, Mahabharata

Subhadrai," Satya said, her arms open wide, "Welcome to the brand-new Hotel K!"

I looked around. It'd been an eight-hour car drive from the field to this shiny, white hotel. It took me a while to realize what was happening. We were in a crowded lobby full of teenagers in red and purple. My eyes bulged.

"They're all KOMC!" Sahana told me in a shrill voice.

I never realized how many of us there were. The lobby was jam-packed, and I could only imagine how many other floors there would be.

"Our room is on the second floor," Satya forced a smile, "Take the elevator there and go to the room marked *Pandavas*."

I nodded, "Yessir."

I ran to the elevator, a childlike curiosity burning inside of me. Amrita smiled slightly and followed me shaking her head with Sahana. I pressed the button marked 'two' and leaned against the walls of the elevator as we rose.

"What did Bhishma say?" Sahana asked.

I looked at her. After Satya had announced that we had to stay locked up in our camps, Rohan and I had met Bhishma.

He made himself clear and said that we *could* leave the camps. We just shouldn't engage in war without him calling it, like Rohan had done.

He also told Rohan off for a long time for doing what he'd done to Myna.

I felt my heart sink.

"He said we had to start recruiting armies in case of war," I said, shrugging, "Although, Rohan already started doing that."

Sahana frowned, "That's it?"

I nodded, "That is *literally* it."

The elevator halted to a stop, and we stepped out onto the cushioned floor. I craned my neck to look down the long line of rooms.

"How big is this place?" I asked, out of breath, as if I'd climbed up the stairs.

Just looking at the long hall made me exhausted.

"Where are we?" I asked.

"Panchalam," Amrita said, "Myna told me that the new hotel was located here, before…"

We fell silent, staring at the long corridor of doors.

"Well," I said, breaking the silence, "We should start looking for the Pandava room."

We passed a bunch of doors with long complicated names engraved on them. If you thought the Greeks and Romans had tough names, wait till you see the Indians. Finally, after what Sahana told me was thirty seconds (it felt like a million hours) we came across the door marked *Pandavas*.

I've loved walking into hotel rooms ever since I was a kid. It's always felt like moving into a new house for a week. This one more so. As we walked in, I bit back a squeal.

"AHHH!" I hollered, "OHMYGODSOHMYGODS!!!!"

Amrita and Sahana stared as I ran around the room.

"LOOK AT THE CEILING!" I shrieked, "IT'S GOT THE PANDAVAS ENGRAVED ON IT!!!"

Amrita sighed, "Great. We'll never get rid of our parents."

Sahana laughed, staring at the large "room". It was the size of a studio with a kitchen, bedrooms and…

"TV!!!" the three of us gasped when we saw it.

On cue, we crammed ourselves onto the couch and switched the large television on.

Midway through a *Disney* movie, there was a knock on the door. I got up and standing at the doorway was Ambika.

"Hey," she smiled, "There wasn't a Kaurava room, so I didn't really know where to go."

A wave of pity crashed over me, "Oh right, okay. Sorry. We're watching *The Little Mermaid*. You want to join?"

She nodded, gratefully.

We went back to the small corner with the TV, but the whole way through the movie, I couldn't help but notice how alone Ambika looked.

SUBHADRAI

HERE SNAKEY, SNAKEY

"King Dhritarashtra and his sons are the forest. O Sanjaya! The Pandavas are the tigers. Do not cut down the forest with its tigers. Do not banish the tigers from the forest." - Krishna

There were two bedrooms with two bunk-beds in each room where we slept. Amrita was in the bottom bunk with me on the top, and Sahana was on another bunkbed below Satya.

Sure, I say *we* slept, but I don't really think I did. I stared at the ceiling for so long, I lost track of time. Ambika was sleeping on the couches in the hall. I guess even despite me acting like I trusted her, I'd never gotten used to her.

There were always those voices asking how we could ever trust her, a daughter of *Duryodhana*?! I don't know *what* I was thinking when I let Ambika join our side, but I knew that this could end two ways; really good, or the end-of-our-lives.

I got up at around one thirty and went to the kitchen. Ambika was still on the couch, fast asleep.

I rummaged through the empty fridge and found a packet of chips. I took it out and walked to the balcony.

Staring at the dot in the distance that was the kingdom of Panchalam, I felt a pang of homesickness. I missed the PS, Abhimanyu, Vedanth, and Akshara. It didn't feel like we were looking for Shrutakarma last week. That felt like another life.

I was about to turn around, but something had wrapped around my leg. I was about to let out a shriek when the black snake coiled around me spoke.

"Calm down," it said, "We're family!"

I stared, "Wh-what?"

"We're family," the snake repeated, "You're a child of the Pandavas, right?"

I nodded. Out of everything that had happened to me so far, this was definitely the weirdest.

"Wonderful! Who is your father?" the snake asked, smiling.

"Um, Bhima," I said, hesitantly.

The snake looked as if it was even more excited, "Really?! I've met your father! Once, when he was poisoned, I saved him!"

I smiled, trying my best not to freak out, "That's nice."

The snake seemed to nod, "Ah well. One of Kunti's ancestors married a naga, basically a snake, so that makes us family."

I stared in shock, "Okay…. I'm related to a lot of people. I'm second cousins with the Kauravas, so… what do you want? Are you some sort of spy or…?"

The Naga flicked its tail in annoyance, "No! I'm here to help! Relatives help each other out, yes?"

I shrugged, "I don't know…"

But it didn't seem to care. It flicked its tail again and my eyes flickered shut as my knees hit the floor.

When I came to, I was aghast. My long braid whipped onto my face as I turned to look around me.

Snakes. So many snakes.

Almost at once they transformed into a half-human, half-snake form.

I shuddered. That was creepier than Rohan's face.

A snake-lady slithered towards us. She looked like a model from waist up but below that was a dark green snake. Perched on her forehead was a tiara of jewels with a serpent engraved on the top, and in the center was a large stone, radiating light.

"Daughter of Bhima," the serpent lady said, "We've heard rumors of war brewing above our realm and felt the urge to help. My sister, Chitrangada, and I'd love to help the great cause of Dharma once more."

My mind was blank. It seemed like nothing she was saying was really entering my brain.

Chitrangada. Snakes. Stones.

I figured I might have been going through a panic attack.

"I've protected the Pandavas from a few sins they've committed on the battlefield," the lady recalled, "And I think it's time I do it again."

Sins. Protection. Battlefield.

Snakes.

"The princess doesn't know what she speaks of!" said a man in the council, "What has Arjuna done for her? It's a waste of our effort to help these mortals!"

Princess. Snake.

I gasped, "Ulupi!"

There was a murmuring in the assembled crowd, but the princess did not smile.

"Yes, I'm Ulupi," said the snake princess, "Wife of Arjuna. We noticed."

I stared. Arjuna had a *lot* of wives, but I'd heard about Ulupi. She was cooler than the others.

She could bring dead people back to life! I remembered her from that show we'd watched all those months ago.

"So, *you* want to help us?" I asked.

"Yes it seems so," Ulupi said, as if she regretted calling me there, "In return for something. We Nagas have been living in the sea for a long time, but unfortunately the sea is no longer fit for us. It has been filled with *garbage*. We need a new home."

I pursed my lips. I didn't know India that well. I most certainly didn't know anything about snake habitats seeing as

I was failing in *seventh* grade. I racked my brain for information about snake homes.

"I know!" I recalled, hitting the side of the head, "We have a forest outside of Indraprastha. The snake Takshaka used to live there, but the Pandavas defeated him! They cut off most of the forest, but it's still pretty big! It's perfect for snakes!"

I hoped I sounded confident, because I'd never seen the forest, and I had no idea what sort of conditions *snake-humans* needed to live. But I *did* know that if these snakes were willing to help us defeat Rohan (if Bhishma ever called a war), it would be amazing.

"There should be enough water for all of us," Ulupi said.

I nodded. If there was one thing I was sure about, it was the water.

"There's a lake."

Ulupi looked at the assembled snakes, "Nagas! We'll fight for the Pandavas and in return they'll give us a home!"

The nagas cheered, and I couldn't help the feeling of pride burning in me. I recruited our first army!

"Hey," I whispered to Ulupi, "You said something about your sister…"

Her hard face broke into a smile, "Yes. She'll help you too, in return for nothing. It's her duty as the king of her kingdom is Arjuna's son."

I laughed. Arjuna had a *lot* of kids.

I bounced on my toes as the nagas dispersed. Two armies! And hopefully more to go. I bet the Kauravas would never get this far *this quickly.*

***

"We already had five armies on our side," Ambika said, "You would know. We had Mathura, Magadha, Madra, Sindhu, and Anga. I bet Rohan has a lot more already. He had a lot of time when you guys went to go look for Shrutakarma. That's why he sent you on that wild goose chase in the first place. Also, a lot of the people who fought for the Kauravas last time are back on their side again, because we actually have a pretty good reason to fight."

"That is?" I asked, ignoring the fact that she included herself in the Kaurava group.

"Well, the Pandavas *were* being pretty obnoxious," Ambika said, wringing her wrists, "Would it *kill* them to let somebody else rule?"

"No," Satya said, sharply, "It'd kill everyone else. Who *knows* what sort of torture the Kauravas would put on the citizens! Plus, the Pandavas rightfully own the throne! Subhadrai is older than Rohan! You can't break the rules."

Ambika shrugged and stayed silent. I was older than Rohan by a month. She probably figured it wasn't that big of a gap.

"You did all that recruiting before we woke up?!" Sahana asked me, incredulously.

I smirked, "I'm a hundred times better than you, Khatri."

Sahana Khatri rolled her eyes and scoffed, "I'm not buying this. Where's the proof?"

"I don't really have any," I said, scratching my head, "So I guess we'll have to wait for a possible war-"

"Possible being the key word," Satya said, impatiently, "We don't even know if there's going to be one! I heard Draupadi and the Pandavas talking. I can't really tell you what, but I doubt that it'll lead up to a war!"

"Well then" I said crossing my arms, "If it's not a war, then what is it? What else could *possibly* decide who gets to control Hastinapura and Indraprastha?!"

Satya looked around uncomfortably, "I don't know."

Ambika looked irritated, "You know, back at the Kaurava camp, we shared secrets. I even told you that my brother was hiding out at Sindhu!"

"Well," Satya said, turning to Ambika menacingly, "Here at the *Pandava* hotel, we stay honest and keep promises. Plus, your brother wasn't there when I went and checked!"

Ambika flinched.

"It's not Ambika's fault," Sahana retorted, "*You* can't even tell us what we're up against. That's not fair to Subhadrai, right?!"

At once, all faces turned to me. I stared back at them, lost.

"I-I don't really...," I looked at them desperately, "Can we go with the flow?"

What sort of future queen didn't have a plan? Me, that's who. I could tell that everyone was slowly losing their confidence.

"Listen to her," Amrita said, encouragingly, "It's only fair that we're as oblivious as the opposition! Subhadrai's just being righteous."

Everyone murmured in agreement.

Satya sighed, and turned, "I've got work to do. If you need me, call. Please don't need me."

And with that she went into the room marked 'Office'. I smiled at Amrita and mouthed *Thanks*.

She stretched, "Okay. What's for breakfast?"

"It better be good," said a voice coming up from the stairs.

All at once, we turned to see-

"You," Sahana fumed.

"Me!" Shrutakarma said, raising his hands in delight, "Hey, sis!"

"Where are your brothers?" Ambika asked anxiously, as if afraid that they would need to pick up another prince from a five-star hotel.

"We're here," Sutasoma said, appearing at the stairwell, "What's for breakfast? I'm starved."

***

Sutasoma stuffed a large samosa into his mouth as if he hadn't eaten for days, "So, we got the nagas on our side? That's good, I guess?"

"Ulupi, you say?' Prativindhya mused, 'Hm… I think she was the wife of Arjuna."

Sahana sighed, "Wow, another one? Who's shocked."

"I am," Shrutakarma said, "My dad married a *snake*? I was never informed about this."

"Legend has it that Arjuna was in exile from Indraprastha for walking into the room where Draupadi and

Yudhishthira were playing dice. He'd gone into a lake to bathe and didn't come out. A snake princess, Ulupi, had brought him to her palace," Abhimanyu said.

Satya's eyes lit up, "I know this story! Ulupi saves Arjuna from the brothers of Bhisma. Then, even *after* being saved, Arjuna gets himself killed by his son. Ulupi then uses a special naga jewel and brings him back to life."

"Yeah, I think I saw that stone," I recalled, "She was wearing it on her crown."

Everyone looked intrigued, but at that moment, there was a crash from the balcony.

"IT WAS AN ACCIDENT!" came a child's voice, "BUT YOU SHOULD PROBABLY COME HERE!"

I sighed, "Okay, let's go."

Sahana smiled, "I swear, our day isn't complete until *some* kid breaks something."

AMBIKA

GOOD LIES DEEP WITHIN

"Friendship never remains in the world in anyone's heart without being worn out, time wears it out, anger destroys it. The poor cannot be the friend of the rich, the unlearned cannot be the friend of the learned, the coward cannot be the friend of the brave." – Drupada, Mahabharata.

I walked down the hallway towards the Pandava room. I hadn't been sleeping there the past few days though. As comfy as that sofa may be, Subhadrai cannot sleep to save her soul. She keeps waking up and walking out to the balcony.

I couldn't sleep through that.

I had a few memories from before the Pandavas started fighting. Back before the meeting that changed everyone's lives, Rohan and I visited the hotel a few times. And as far as I can remember, no one's ever stayed in the Krishna room.

An old friend of mine, a son of Krishna named Shishir said that it was like that because the castle was far more comfortable. Additionally, not even a fourth of Krishna's children would fit in that room.

So, based on this fact, I entered the room to find a ginormous luxury apartment that was probably meant to exist in some expensive state-of-the-art hotel in Dubai, but ended up here.

Not to mention, the beds in the Krishna room were so much more comfortable than that couch in the Pandava room.

Of course, my stay in the room wasn't a complete secret...

"Hi!" came a voice behind me.

I whirled around to see a young boy, Myna's brother Vijay, standing behind me.

"Bye," I said, turning around, rolling my eyes.

"You're such a meanie to me," said the nine-year-old, falling in line with me, "You're so nice to the Pandavas."

I sighed, "Haven't we talked about this before?"

"Yeah," Vijay said, "But I don't understand what you mean!"

"What do you not understand?" I sighed.

"You said the Pandavas haven't met you yet," Vijay said, scrunching his forehead, "What is *that* supposed to mean."

I laughed, "It means exactly that. I have to go, kid. You keep thinking about that."

Vijay shot me a withering glare that in my personal opinion, a nine-year-old should not be capable of.

I disappeared into the Pandava room, leaving Vijay to wander off.

"Hey!" I said, "What's up?"

Subhadrai smiled, "Hey! We were just talking about how we should start recruiting more armies."

I stared. About *time*.

"So," Satya said, squinting at me, "Do you have any ideas?"

"Dwaraka," I blurted, "The Kauravas had a major advantage because they had the Dwaraka army in the last war! We might be able to beat them to it!"

Satya glanced at Sahana skeptically, "Alright. It's a nice idea, but it's not realistic. Your brother probably already has Dwaraka. You mentioned that he had Mathura, yes?"

"He most probably doesn't have Dwaraka," I said, "But in case."

I pulled out my phone and rang up a certain someone who was sure to know.

"Hey Ambika," came a voice from the other end, "I told you not to bother me until you got back on- "

"Hi Nisata," I said, cutting him short, "Has Rohan called dibs on the Dwaraka army yet?"

Nisata went silent, "He's trying. He keeps getting an appointment with the king, but Vasudeva keeps postponing it. I guess he's waiting for the Pandavas…Are *you* coming?"

I hung up the phone. It wasn't my job to answer that question.

"So, are we?" I asked Satya.

She looked a tad bit more hopeful, "Okay. We'll send Subhadrai. She's already done this recruiting thing."

"Finally," Subhadrai said, pumping her fist into the air, "I can't *wait* to see who this Nisata dude is!"

She'd be shocked. Shishir (one of the sons of Krishna), Nisata and I used to be inseparable. In fact, they taught me everything about… well, everything. Nisata was not the mysterious know-it-all figure everyone thought he was.

I sat down on the couch that used to be my bed, "Is that it?"

"Having only Dwaraka isn't going to help us at all," Satya said, looking at Subhadrai, "You have any ideas?"

"Well," Subhadrai perked up, "We could send Ambika somewhere."

Satya looked as if she'd rather send Peppa Pig, "Um… where?"

"How about Ayodhya?" Subhadrai decided, "There's no way they'd *ever* say no! You saw how *cheerful* the whole kingdom was that day!"

Subhadrai's positivity didn't move anyone. Satya glanced at Shyamala who didn't seem convinced.

"It's worth a try," Amrita shrugged.

Satya turned and scrutinized me. Then, after what seemed like a millennium, she sighed, "Okay, let's do it."

***

I did *not* sign up for this. Debating with two stubborn princes was *way* above my pay grade (And I wasn't even getting paid). Unfortunately, that was *exactly* what I found myself doing.

"I *am* on the Pandavas' side!" I insisted, "I swear!"

"Where's the proof?!" asked the prince, Shatrugna.

They hadn't even let me inside the palace. We were in the stables, surrounded by horse poo.

I hesitated, "Well, they didn't give me any."

"That proves our point," the other prince, Bharatha said, triumphantly.

"No, it doesn't!" I said, rolling my eyes, "I could take you to the hotel! You could ask *them*."

"I'm not going somewhere with a random stranger," Shatrugna huffed, "Haven't you read *Little Red Riding Hood?* Who did you say you were from again?"

I groaned, and started explaining again as if they were kindergarteners, "I'm Ambika and I'm from *KOMC*. I'm on the Pandavas' side! *They* want to recruit you for a hypothetical war."

Who would ever want to recruit these people? They'd sent me on a hopeless quest.

Bharatha and Shatrugna exchanged wary looks, and Shatrugna asked, "Who is your father? You look familiar, so if you're from KOMC, then who are your parents?"

I smiled unnaturally. Revealing I was a Kaurava was not the best way to gain trust.

"Ha!" Bharatha said, "You aren't a KOMC! Are you from one of those fan clubs?"

Who'd make a fan club for these guys?

"I'm a school friend!" I said, desperately.

"No, she *is* a KOMC, Shatrugna said, ignoring me, "But I bet she's from the Kauravas' side. Are you from Chedi?"

I wasn't *that* bad, "No! My dad is Duryodhana, okay? But I joined the Pandavas! Don't freak."

The brothers stared at me and then… they freaked. In half a second there were two swords pointed at my throat.

"Woah," I chuckled nervously, "Calm down."

"If you speak, you die," Bharatha said, brandishing his sword at me, "Leave."

I looked at the swords on both sides of me, "Kinda hard to do at the moment."

"Do the light-travel thing," Shatrugna growled in a way that actually made that phrase sound scary, "And if we ever see you here again, consider yourself at Yama's door."

Yama was the god of death, by the way.

I nodded deciding that it wasn't worth arguing about, and light-traveled back to the hotel's doorstep.

Don't worry, Shatrughna, I thought, *Satya will send me there for you.*

"They said no?" Satya exclaimed, frustrated, "How could they- You didn't tell them you were on our side?!"

"THEY WANTED PROOF!" I protested, "YOU DIDN'T GIVE ME ANY!"

"I-" Satya frantically thought of an excuse, "Can't you make something up?"

"Oh, now the granddaughter of the *god of righteousness* wants me to *lie*?" I asked.

All of a sudden, I felt my eyes burn.

Who did the Pandavas think they were to boss me around like this?

Who did Bharatha and Shatrugna think they were to kick me out like that?

Satya stared at me with surprising worry, "Are you okay?"

I scowled, biting back my tears, "Yeah."

A tear rolled down.

Stupid tears.

Satya opened her mouth, and I whipped around to find Sahana walking in. She looked at me then at Satya, a faltering smile on her face.

"What happened?"

I ran away before I heard her response.

SUBHADRAI

IS LOYALTY THAT HARD?

"Pleasant looks, cheerful heart and sweet words are due to a guest. Rising up, the host should advance towards the guest; he should offer him a seat and duly worship him. This is the eternal Dharma." – Mahabharata

What happened?" Sahana asked, as Ambika fled the room.

Satya winced, "She didn't recruit Ayodhya."

Sahana frowned, "So? That's okay."

I glared at Satya, "*She* didn't think so."

"I'm still not over the fact that Satya told Ambika to lie," Amrita said, her eyes wide.

"What?!" Sahana asked, shocked, "Your *name* means truth!"

Satya buried her head in her hands as she sunk into the couch, "Shut up. I was stressed."

"You ready?" Shyamala asked me, "I have a good feeling about this one. Third time's the charm."

I blinked, "What?"

"You're going to Dwaraka," Satya said, looking up at me, "Now."

***

"Hello?" I called.

I stood at the Dwaraka front gate. There was a main gate that wasn't guarded at all. I peered into the garden and saw five guards at the front gate. That explained the easy entrance.

I decided to walk over.

"Hello?" I asked, walking towards the front gate, "I need to meet the…"

My voice faltered. There was a boy, about eleven, already speaking to the guards.

"Um, who are you?" the boy asked, looking back at me.

The dark black hair under his blue baseball cap, along with his tan skin reminded me of Abhimanyu.

"Subhadrai," I said, "You?"

"Subhadrai is a common name," The boy said, crossing his arms, "My aunt's name is Subhadra. What's your last name?"

Talk about nosy.

"Anand," I said, slowly.

The boy's eyes lit up, "The daughter of Bhima?"

I couldn't help but smile with pride, "Yeah."

"Come in!" he said, leading me past the helpless guards, "I'm Nisata."

I halted, "*You*?"

Nisata smirked with a childish pride, "You've heard of me?"

I shrugged, "Kinda."

"From Abhimanyu?" Nisata asked.

I recalled Abhimanyu joining our gang to find Shrutakarma.

I nodded.

"He was a source."

"He's my cousin," Nisata explained, "He tends to make me seem a whole lot bigger than I am."

"Yeah, I guess," I agreed, "I expected you to look-"

"Like James Bond?" Nisata struck a lame pose.

"Uh, no," I laughed, "More like a human Pink Panther."

Okay, yes. I was expecting a James Bond, but I wasn't letting *him* know that.

"Very funny," His face turned serious, "I bet you want to see my grandfather."

"That depends," I said, turning serious too, "Who is your grandfather?"

Nisata looked shocked, "Oh, come on! Vasudeva! The king of Dwaraka!"

"In that case, yes", I nodded, expertly, "Yes, I would like to see your king."

Nisata looked at me with suspicion, probably shocked that an idiot like me was sent to recruit a whole kingdom. Little did he know what an expert I was.

He led me to the throne room where I spotted -

"Abhimanyu?"

He stood beside an old man sitting on an enormous throne who was talking to a bunch of people at once, so he didn't hear me.

"That's the king," Nisata pointed at the aged man on the throne with a tall crown, "And *that's* my father."

He pointed to a buff man next to Abhimanyu who was talking to a lady next to him. Surprisingly, everyone in the room looked a bit familiar.

Especially the lady.

"That's my aunt, Subhadra," Nisata said, "She's the original Subhadra, the sister of Krishna, and-"

"Abhimanyu's mother," I recalled, "Who's your father?"

"Balarama," Nisata said, casually.

My jaw may or may not have hit the floor.

Balarama had a son?!

Balarama was the brother of Krishna, and the incarnation of Lord Vishnu. I thought that the gods didn't reincarnate on Brahma's command…

I told him that.

"Yeah, but Lord Krishna sent his siblings to watch over us," Nisata said.

As far as I was concerned, both Krishna and Balarama were gods, and Subhadra, a goddess.

So, both Nisata and Abhimanyu were demigods.

"AHH! OH MY GOD! YOU'RE A DEMIGOD! HE'S A DEMIGOD? I…wh-" I squealed.

Nisata didn't seem that proud, "Well your dad is an indirect son of Vayu, so I don't get why you're freaking out."

Oh yeah…

"I guess," I said, "But that's different."

Nisata smiled, "Let me take you to the king."

He strode over to the throne and the king looked up from his conversation.

"Nisata!" he said, "It's good you're here. I've been meaning to-"

The king spotted me.

"Who's this?" he asked, his expression going dark.

"This is the daughter of Bhima. The new queen," Nisata said, "Subhadrai."

The room went silent, so I decided to say something.

I cleared my throat dramatically, "On behalf of the Pandavas, and the KOMC," I glanced at the goddess Subhadra, "We want to recruit you."

Not the best choice of words, but I thought it sounded cool.

The king glanced at Balarama as he said, "We were told there wasn't going to be a war."

"Yeah. Well, maybe," I said, "But there *might* be, and we need to be ready."

"It would be a waste of our time and resources if we prepared an army that's never going to be used," Balarama pointed out.

My stupid mind thought of Ambika running away in tears when she'd failed.

I gulped, "I mean…you…"

"She wants our loyalty," Nisata said, "Can't you give them that?"

The king eyed me, "What other kingdom is in your army?"

I remembered Satya's disappointed face.

No one.

Except for that son of Arjuna I'd recruited, but I didn't remember her name.

"We went for the best first," I grinned, lying, because that's one thing school taught me "But we have people who will be recruiting Ayodhya soon."

The king seemed convinced.

(Flattery was awesome. Try it at home, kids.)

He turned to Balarama and whispered. Subhadra gave me a hopeful smile. I glanced at Nisata who was staring at his father expectantly.

Balarama withdrew from his hushed conversation and looked at his son. His stony face cracked a smile, and he said something that looked like, *Alright.* But it could have also been *Yeah, right.*

The king's gaze fell upon me, and he gave me a nod, "You have our loyalty."

ROHAN

FEAR

"Once war has been undertaken, no peace is made by pretending there is no war." – Duryodhana, Mahabharata

I frowned at the sword before me. Its hilt had my father's emblem– a roaring lion– engraved on it. I would've expected my father to want me to have it, but he didn't seem that keen.

Despite all the efforts to turn me into a younger version of him, (a scheme I was aware of) the fact that I'd killed Myna had seemed to have made him distance himself from me.

It had made me distance myself from me too.

It'd been *months* since I'd let myself sleep. In the beginning it was the Syamantaka gem. Now, it was the guilt.

I put the sword down, not looking at my father, "I'll think about it."

He didn't say anything, so I took that as a sign to leave but when I was halfway out the door, he called my name.

I stopped knowing that if I didn't turn around it would probably make me feel worse. I braced myself to turn around and hear him tell me how disappointed he was, but instead my feet sprinted up the staircase and into my bed.

I leaned back against the bedframe, my eyes closed. I shouldn't have done that, but if I'd stayed, he wouldn't only mention Myna… he'd talk about Ambika too.

Stupid Ambika… She'd just left! And I'd trusted her!

Did she realize how much that one move had done? I sunk deeper into the bed, groaning.

The *only* person who I knew was on *my* side had gone! She'd gone running to a random American girl who couldn't wield anything more than a sword.

I got up, staring at the mirror in front of me. On the glass was a sticker that read 'Future King' with a picture of a seven-year-old me grinning. My father had stuck it there before the fight with the Pandavas had happened.

I clenched my jaw. I *would* be the king. I wasn't going to give up my throne for a loser like Subhadrai.

I glared at the image, but it just grinned back. Now, the kid who'd posed for that picture wasn't excited to sit on the throne. He was just a shadow following his father's footsteps.

He was now a murderer.

I walked away from the mirror in disgust.

"Dude!" came Anish's voice from downstairs, "We're going out for dinner! If you want to come, come, but I want you to know that it would be great if I could get through this evening without seeing your face!"

"*Anish*! Stop that," cried his mother, "Rohan, dear, come down."

I looked back at the mirror as if the picture was going to tell me what to do. There was no point sulking about how Ambika had left someone who trusted her anymore. She wasn't here. Myna was still dead.

I walked out, dragging my feet down the stairs.

Anish's grandmother stood at the foot of the staircase waiting.

"You know what that Subhadrai girl did?" she asked me.

I stared at her in quiet rage.

The *'Subhadrai'* girl. The *charming* new queen who knew *everything*. Everyone seemed to have forgotten that it was me who'd trained my entire life. Whatever Subhadrai knew now, I knew when I was seven.

"Oh, leave it," Anish's mom said, shaking her head, "He doesn't need to be even more demotivated. The poor dear is hardly eating anything anymore."

"Why is that a bad thing?" Anish asked, "I get more."

I glared at him. Honestly, I don't think I would hate him that much if Ambika hadn't hated him first. The thought of that made me even angrier.

I didn't even know who I was angry at anymore, "I'm not coming for dinner."

"*Very* funny," Bhanumati said, grabbing my hand, "Come on. It's Anish's birthday."

No wonder he was feeling extra good about himself today.

"No way," I said, "Happy Birthday, genius. Enjoy another year of being useless."

With that I stormed out to the limousine where my father was waiting for me.

"Are you hungry?" He asked.

I shook my head without looking at him.

"Neither am I," he said, as though he was trying to make me talk (he must've spoken with my mother), "I've also realized that I don't really like this Anish character."

I snorted trying hard not to break a grin, "Congratulations. I realized *that* when I first met him."

"What do you think about ditching the dinner?" Duryodhana asked, "Your mom will take time to come out, anyways. D'you want to go for a walk?"

I shrugged. As much as I didn't want to deal with his disappointment, it was better than hearing Anish boast about his awesomeness.

"Fine," I said, following him.

He walked a few paces before he turned to me.

"I know you've been killing yourself over how you killed Myna," Duryodhana said, "Don't worry. Everything happens for a reason, and if you're going to be king, you've got to be prepared to split a soul from its body."

That did *not* make me feel better at all.

I didn't want to kill. I didn't want to have seen Myna's scared expression before I lunged at her.

Technically, I'd gone to the Pandava camp to ask for more time to gather armies right before the war. I knew that Bhishma would give us time anyways. I don't know what got into me. I saw the gem with Subhadrai and in half a second, Myna was dead.

I also knew that without Myna, Subhadrai's team would be a wreck

I wasn't wrong either. According to our spy, they'd recruited one army so far.

Then again, I had a head start because I sent the girls to find Shrutakarma.

"How many kingdoms do we have now?" Duryodhana asked, as if he was reading my mind.

"Seven," I responded.

"Rohan," Duryodhana said, as he kept walking, "You were meant for this, okay? Trust me. I didn't train you so that Bhima's daughter could come and sit on the throne. Especially not if a dead lady told her it was the right thing to do."

Well, a desperate villain had told *me* to. I felt bitter in my mouth, and I'm pretty sure it wasn't because of that vegetable my mother made me eat that morning.

"You have competition now, Rohan," Duryodhana said, cracking his knuckles, "And you are far more capable than her! You're the only one who can do this right."

I rolled my eyes. Now where had I heard that before?

If that was even remotely true, then why was Subhadrai, who didn't even know she was related to the

Pandavas a year ago, suddenly winning the hearts of everyone around her.

The second we stepped out of the palace; the people on the street straightened up as if we would kill them for slouching.

I wondered if that's what my father wanted.

I knew that Uncle Kamsa would've done that. But he was dead. Is that what fate did to people like us?

Were we made to die just like the people who'd died because of us?

I bit my tongue.

Was *Subhadrai* going to be my death?

Most importantly, would she rule my kingdom?

The kingdom that everyone had constantly told me I was born for.

"Fear," Duryodhana said, jerking me out of my thoughts in a low whisper, "Fear is how we have to rule. They'll never trust us again."

I looked up at him. Of *course* they wouldn't. After everything he'd done. He should never have listened to his uncle.

What a hypocrite I was. *I'd* listened to his uncle. I wondered if Duryodhana knew.

We stopped in front of a forgery and the blacksmith's wife fled into the house as the man outside looked at us, his hands trembling.

"What weapons do you make?" Duryodhana asked, curiously, his voice booming.

I knew that there was no threat in his voice, but the man would never bother noticing that.

Fear…

"S-sir, w-we do j-jewelry," the man said, "N-not weap-p-pons," the man shivered, glancing at the dagger on my belt.

I covered it with my maroon jacket and looked away.

This was how I had to rule.

Nothing would ever change the way the people looked at us Kauravas.

We were no more than villains, weren't we?

SUBHADRAI

WHATEVER HAPPENED, NOT MY FAULT

"Anger is, in this world, the root of the destruction of mankind" – Yudhisthira, Mahabharata

I light-traveled into total chaos as Shyamala, Amrita and Satya were all screaming at Sahana. Something about some moldy sandwich and how she hadn't washed her hands.

I tried to balance myself, because I still hadn't become an expert at light-traveling, and I tripped over Ambika's bag that she'd left there. As it toppled, a sheet of paper fell out.

I picked it up, and then Satya started screaming at me, because it's illegal to read other people's letters. Amrita was screaming because Sahana hadn't washed her hands. Shyamala was screaming because I was back.

But I wasn't screaming. The letter had made me go numb.

Hey Sis

I know you're pretty frustrated with Dad, but you've survived for 11 years with him. Kind of. Plus, he's sort of understanding how the palace is without you. It's quiet. It's clean. ~~No one has a headache....~~

Anyways, that's not important. Here's what you need to know; I'm awesome. Yeah, I guess you already knew that, but I mean it even more now. We got Mathura, Magadha, Madra, Sindhu, Anga. Chedi, Gandhara etc., etc.

Just kidding, that's all I got.

But I bet it's a lot better than what the Pandavas have! And I'd do better with your bargaining. Just think about it.

You're so much better than the Pandavas.

Love, Rohan

"SHUT UP!" I screamed, "It's from Rohan!"

That did it.

The room quieted down and I could finally hear my thoughts.

I started to wish the room had stayed chaotic because I didn't like them.

Ambika could've already sent a letter back to Rohan accepting his invitation. I checked the date.

It was a week ago. That was a week *after* Myna had been murdered.

Ambika had gotten the message during her stay here, and she hadn't told us. Amrita and I sent letters to each other when we were angry at each other. Normally, it doesn't take a week to receive a response.

Generally, ten minutes, seeing that all the anger had to cool down first.

But Ambika was still here, so she *must've* said no.

With that hopeful note, I spoke once more, "He asked Ambika to join him."

My ears were *never* going to be the same again. At once, Satya was screaming at me to give her the paper, and when I didn't, she grabbed it from me, and Amrita and Shyamala immediately shut up and stood behind her craning their necks to see the crumpled up piece of paper.

"Stop!" I said, "We have *no* idea where she is. She could be coming here right now, and when she sees us fussing over the paper, she's going to be furious."

Satya looked up at me, "Ambika won't be coming here anytime soon."

"Why is that?"

"Classes are going on," Satya said, matter-of-factly.

I frowned, "What?"

"Classes," Satya said, "You guys don't need to attend, because I assumed you might be busy, although I was *terribly* mistaken."

She glanced at Sahana who guiltily shrugged. Satya had caught her watching YouTube shorts while she was supposed to be practicing archery.

"What sort of classes?" Amrita asked, intrigued.

"Oh, you know," Satya shrugged, "Archery, sword-fighting, spear-wielding. And also, stuff like math, English, Sanskrit, science, because most of the people here no longer go to school anymore. It's a full-time war."

I thought it over. Classes…

"And can we join these classes?" I asked.

Sahana gave me a death-glare, but Satya looked overjoyed, "Yup! Do you want to?"

I shrugged, "Not really."

"We have sword fighting, painting," Satya said, desperately, "Sanskrit."

"Does anyone even know Sanskrit?" Sahana asked.

"It's an official second language in a bunch of schools in India," Shyamala said.

Satya ignored the question, "You guys aren't that busy. You'll love it, I promise."

"Can we talk about this later," I asked, because Sahana was giving me a look that said that if I ever agreed, I might be stabbed by a certain someone on my way to the fridge at midnight.

I don't know why, but I was scared of that.

Satya hesitantly let the topic go, "Anyways, classes only have five-minute breaks, so the chances of her coming during those are low."

She picked up the letter again and started to read. Sahana quickly scooted over to her and peeked over Satya shoulder. Shyamala scowled.

"Read it out loud," she said, but her request remained unheard as Satya's eyes darted back and forth in shock.

Satya looked up at me midway, "Check her bag and see if there's anything else."

"Like?" I asked.

"I don't know. Letters after this?" Satya suggested.

Amrita frowned, "Postal service here sucks."

"Tell me about it," Shyamala agreed, "I didn't even know it *existed*."

"Just check!" Satya ordered.

I nodded and stuck my hand into her bag and rummaged around. That's when the door swung open and Ambika stood there, a pizza box in one hand, grinning.

AMBIKA

WHERE DO WE START?

**"They that are desirous of victory do not so much conquer by might and prowess as by truth compassion, piety, and virtue. Fight without any arrogance, for victory is certain to be where righteousness is." –
Sanjaya, Mahabharata**

I looked at Subhadrai, her hand halfway in my bag. The pizza I'd bought fell to the floor.

So much for *trusting* me. I glanced at Satya and saw her holding a sheet of paper. It took me a second to recognize it.

I felt my face flush with anger.

"How *dare* you?!" I cried, glaring at Satya, "And to think I *trusted* you!"

Satya winced as I snatched the letter from her hand.

My letter.

From *my* brother.

She had *no* right to read that.

I tried to steel my nerves.

"Really, Subhadrai?" I turned to the daughter of Bhima.

She opened her mouth, then closed it.

I turned to Sahana, who looked as shocked as I was.

I scoffed, "Wow."

I looked around at the children of the Pandavas. As sneaky, as disloyal, as greedy as the Kauravas.

Well, two can play that game.

"Well done, Anand," I snapped at Subhadrai, "You've just lost your last fleeting chance at winning."

Subhadrai's mouth dropped open as I grabbed the bag from her and stomped out.

Slammed the door shut, I rammed into Vijay.

"Move it," I growled, my teacup of anger growing into an ocean.

Rohan always said that when I got angry at one thing, I got angry at everything. I have no idea what he was talking about.

I stormed into the room, and then the hurricane hit.

I ripped a canopy of a bed, too furious to see anything.

After kicking the bed, I threw an expensive-looking vase at the floor and started punching my pillow.

"I hate them," I muttered, with every blow, on the verge of tears, "They *suck*! They-"

"Woah, Princess," said a smooth voice from behind me, "Chill."

I whipped around, my undone hair falling on my face. No way.

My knees sunk further into the bed I was on as I stared at the boy with the British accent near the door.

"That *is* mine," he said, gesturing to the pillow, "But you can have it if you like."

He sat down next to me and stared at the wall. After all the time there I'd forgotten whose room it was.

"So," he said, "This feels nice, huh? After all this time there... Have you had spoken with Nisata?

I shook my head even though I had.

"Oh, good," he laughed, "I thought you guys abandoned me."

I kept staring at the wall.

This wasn't happening.

I was asleep.

It was a nightmare. Everything I didn't want to happen was happening.

He nudged me, "So, we're all on the Pandavas' side now, eh?"

I shook my head, "No."

He frowned, "What?"

"I hate them," I repeated, glancing at the pillow with a small crater in it.

"Oh, yes," he glanced at the pillow too, "I recall. So, you're going back to your brother and spilling all your juicy secrets?"

I glanced at him, uncertainly.

He wasn't looking.

"Shishir," I said.

He turned to me, "Yes?"

"I don't want to stay here, but I don't want to go there," I said, a sob building up in my throat.

"Well," he said, smiling, "Like Nisata always said, *When you're stuck between a rock and a hard place, build a house right where you are and stay there*.'"

I frowned, "What's that supposed to mean?"

"I don't know," he shrugged, "That bloke is weird."

I laughed but it came out like a sob. Right where you are… I pictured myself on the throne and I don't know why, but it felt right. Maybe because I'd seen both Rohan and Subhadrai rule.

I took a deep breath.

"You mean *I* should rule?" I asked.

"Woah, easy. I never said that," he shrugged, nonchalantly, "It's up to you."

"Well then, watch me sit on the throne of Hastinapura," I said, hastily, "I'm going to do this ruling thing a whole lot better than them."

"You mean the Pandavas?" Shishir asked, stretching with a yawn.

"And the Kauravas."

There was a beat of silence as he straightened his back. He was going to laugh.

Shishir knew me. Both he and Nisata knew that I couldn't rule a kingdom.

They would die from laughter if I tried.

I could picture it already.

You? Rule a kingdom?

Nice joke. Where's Rohan?

But Shishir turned to me curiously.

I decided to keep blabbering, "I know I can do it. I don't know where to start though. Rohan recruited three kingdoms. Subhadrai has one and a half, if you count Ayodhya."

"Well," Shishir shrugged, "You can recruit me."

SUBHADRAI

SECOND GRADE IS TRAUMATIC

"Passion, engagement, skill and policy – these are the means to accomplish objectives." – Ashwatthama, Mahabharata

Oof," Sahana said, closing the door. I got up and walked into the bathroom, my mind racing. Satya opened her mouth to say something, but Amrita signaled her to shut up. I closed the door behind me as I heard Amrita tell Satya I was sensitive.

I would've cried if she hadn't said that, but instead it made me roll my eyes.

Me? Sensitive? Why didn't she step into my place for a second?

Then I remembered what just happened. I stared at the tiled walls, my heart beating in fright.

I'd lost *Ambika.*

If she joined the Kauravas because we wanted to read a letter, then…

I couldn't live with that. I had to find her.

I opened the door and walked out without a word. Sahana was eating the pizza that Ambika had dropped. Satya stared at me, and both our eyes met.

I whipped around and left.

I stormed to the Dwaraka room where I knew Ambika had been staying, but I heard voices and stopped.

Maybe it was Rohan.

I stepped back, about to ask someone if anyone had seen who went into the room when the door opened, and she walked out.

A boy followed her, but it wasn't Rohan. He looked older than me with long dark hair falling across his forehead and white shirt.

He looked like Abhimanyu.

He turned to me, smirked, and whispered something to Ambika.

She kept walking.

"Ambika!" I called desperately.

No response. She stepped in front of the elevator and pressed the button. I stared, my heart pounding against my chest. I should've run to stop her, but I didn't.

Ambika turned around and her stone hard face didn't turn in my direction even once. I watched as the door closed.

No.

This couldn't be happening. I refused to believe it. I ran down the stairs calling Ambika's name, but when I got into the lobby, she wasn't there.

I was about to turn and go back to the room when I heard a scream.

I frowned and halted.

"HELP!"

I walked out the hotel and into the street looking around.

"HELP!"

Running towards the sound of the voice, it didn't take me long to find the source.

There was a dense crowd surrounding someone.

I pushed through and spotted a kid, barely breathing, his parents screaming for help.

I don't know what came over me, but I knelt down trying to help.

"What happened?" I asked.

The mother was sobbing so hard she couldn't speak. She managed to let out one word though.

"Snake."

I breathed in sharply. I couldn't turn away now. I told the mother to move and picked the child up. I hoped he was still alive.

I ran to the hotel, praying that I would find the nagas again.

Swinging the door open, I set the child down in the lobby. Holding his hand, I pictured the place where the nagas had taken me and light-traveled.

I opened my eyes and found myself, once more, in the undersea cavern.

"It's the queen!" I heard a naga cry.

Ignoring that I'd been called 'queen', I rushed the child towards Ulupi's throne. She stared at me as if I was wearing bright neon at a funeral.

"Can you heal him?" I asked, out of breath.

Ulupi raised her eyebrow at the child, "Who *is* this?"

I paused.

"I don't know," I said.

The queen stared at me in confusion and then nodded in assent, "Give."

She took the child into a room guarded by two huge cobras, so I decided not to follow. Instead, I paced the throne room eavesdropping on what the nagas were saying.

"She doesn't know!"

"Why would she bring him?"

"She must care for *some* reason."

"Why would she care?"

Ulupi came almost immediately holding the hand of the boy who seemed perfectly fine.

"The venom was slow," She reassured me, "He's fine."

"Thank you," I said, taking the boy's hand.

He smiled up at me and I smiled back in relief. What was I thinking? What was I supposed to do if he'd died?

I was about to leave when Ulupi told me to stop.

"When you first recruited me, I had my doubts," she admitted, "But now, I know, you will make a wonderful queen. I am willingly under your leadership, Subhadrai. Rohan may rule well under fear, but you… you rule with care."

And she bowed.

One by one the nagas followed, their heads almost sweeping the floor.

I stared at them, my brain refusing to accept who they were bowing for.

"Where's my mom?" the boy asked, groggily, yanking me out of the moment.

"Thank you," I repeated to the nagas, gesturing for the boy to wait, and I light-travelled away.

When I appeared in the lobby, the child's mother let out a cry and grabbed her son.

I stepped back as the rest of the crowd cheered and nudged each other in shock.

The father tussled the boy's hair and looked at me, "Thank you, your majesty."

We weren't even in Indraprastha, but here this guy was, calling me the queen.

I smiled. Maybe this throne was worth fighting for after all.

***

I swung the door of the *Pandava* room open, expecting to see everyone scream at me for losing Ambika, but there was no one to see.

The room was empty.

I walked over to the window, staring at the pizza box lying on the tattered couch. I pulled the light blue curtains open and peered out the window. A mosquito flew in front of my face, and I swatted it away.

"I swear," I muttered, angrily, "The only problem with India is the mosquitoes."

Anyone who's come from America to India would agree.

I glanced at the ground through the glass. There stood the PD, gathered around something on the floor. The stable girl, Tara was huddled at the corner of the stable with the horses, pale with fright. It was with a jolt that I realized how old she was. She couldn't have been more than seven. Why was she here?

I took the elevator back down and walked over to the group. They were huddled over a patch of grass. I cleared my throat and Amrita looked up.

"Where's Ambika?" She asked, raising her eyebrow.

I shrugged, trying not to look, "She left."

Amrita frowned, "Where did she go?"

I shrugged again, not being much help.

She rolled her eyes and looked back at the ground. Then back up.

"Why are we here again?" She asked Sahana.

Sahana looked up and Satya and Shyamala followed, confused looks on their faces. They turned to me.

"Let's go and find Ambika," Satya suggested.

"Why are we here again?" Amrita repeated.

"Tara freaked out about something," Sahana said, "and she pointed here, so we came here. Then Subhadrai came."

"So, what happened?" I asked, swatting a mosquito.

Sahana shrugged.

I turned around to leave when somebody laughed. I whipped around, annoyed, but saw that the rest of them were looking in the same direction as I was in fear.

"What *happened?*" I asked for what felt like the hundredth time.

Sahana took a step back, then I saw it. What I'd thought was an oddly shaped cloud in the sky seemed to be moving right at us. With a start I realized what it was. Bees. Dark, black bees. A shudder went up my spine as the cloud of bees landed before me in the shape of a lady. And right where there should've been more bees were two eyes.

I whimpered.

Very heroic, I know.

I've hated bees ever since one of them stung a kid named William during recess in second grade.

But now I realized I hated bees with huge white eyes even more.

Then the bees parted, and I realized that the bees didn't own the eyes. It was worse. It belonged to a woman.

Right at the center of the black fog-like swarm was a pretty, nice-looking lady. That scared me. I stumbled back as she came closer, but Shyamala grabbed the neck of my shirt.

"Oh, no you don't," she snarled.

Satya grabbed her spear from its little sheath on her back. I decided to pull out my sword too, as Amrita balled her fists. Her maze was probably in the room.

There was a soft buzzing noise as the bees formed two clouds next to the lady.

"Where are the Pandavas?" she asked, softly, "The girls."

"Why?" Satya asked.

The lady eyed her, realization sparking in her eyes, "Because, Daughter of Yudhishthira, I would like to join your side and sting the life out of Duryodhana."

I glanced at Satya in shock, "Um, that sounds good."

"Yes, doesn't it?" The lady said, "I'm Brahmari, goddess of black bees, insects, bugs and other cool stuff."

My jaw dropped.

Another goddess.

A *celestial* being. Rukmini was too much for me to take. This was way cooler than Nisata being a demigod.

Even if I wanted to say no, could I?

"Oh, don't be so shocked," Brahmari said.

Her voice was a low hum as if a bunch of bees were talking.

"You will meet many more celestial beings," she laughed, "Although you may not have captured the interest of kingdoms on Earth, many from Indra Loka have been inspired."

Indra Loka.

Indra's abode.

I felt like fainting. Indra was the god of *gods*. Technically he was also Sahana's grandfather.

It's complicated.

My celestial grandfather was Vayu the god of wind.

Not as cool as Indra, but when you're related to a god, you shouldn't get picky.

"That's," I looked at Satya again, "nice."

"Isn't it?" Brahmari repeated, "So, what do you say?"

"Yes," I said, glad to see that the others nodded quickly.

Brahmari clapped in delight. She didn't seem like she ruled over any creepy crawlies, more like fairies and Barbie dolls.

Brahmari smiled at me, then at the others one by one.

"May the side of righteousness win," she said, proudly and the bees surrounded her once more and she floated away, to become a black dot in the distance.

"Well," Satya said, after a beat of silence, "It's been a long day, and I think you should get some sleep."

I shuddered.

Sleep.

That was the last thing I wanted to do.

I trudged to my canopy bed, and sunk into the mattress, sitting there for a while as one by one all the other PD dropped off to sleep.

I leaned back against the wall at around one o' clock, sighing.

Something told me that tomorrow was going to suck.

SUBHADRAI

THE NEW ARMY

"A man becometh a foe by speaking words that are unpardonable." - Duryodhana, Mahabharata

Satya shook me again, "Wake up."

I groaned and hit my head on the wall behind me.

My eyes snapped open, "What?"

"You're going to be late," Satya said, standing straight, walking over to Sahana's bed where she lay drooling.

"For what?" I asked, getting up, rubbing my head.

"Class," Satya said, and I wondered if she knew how vague she was being.

I understood though, "You mean those KOMC classes with the Sanskrit and all that?"

"Exactly," Satya said, "And you don't want to be late."

She tossed me a KOMC uniform. A purple shirt and red pants, just like the one in California.

I sighed and got up, acting annoyed, but I *was* excited.

And from the way Sahana stared at Satya when she told her, I could tell I'd be the only one.

Sahana refused to wash her face, and inspired the others so it ended up looking like Satya's brought three homeless kids and me to a five-star hotel.

We went up to the fiftieth floor and walked over to the room marked 7B. Satya turned the knob and gave Sahana, Amrita, Shyamala, and me a thumbs up as she swung the door open.

"Welcome," Satya said smiling, "to Indian school."

Sahana went in first, followed by Amrita.

The teacher had a wooden whiteboard eraser raised as if she was about to bang it on the table.

And when the class burst into an excited whisper, she did.

"We have new students joining us from America," the teacher said, with hardly a smile.

I glanced at Satya nervously. No doubt in America, the teacher would've been a bit more hyped.

We walked in and sat in the four empty seats.

Satya smiled as if we had no idea what we were walking into.

***

"Um, miss?" I raised my hand, "What chapter are we doing?"

The guy in front of me snickered, "Yo, Aarav. Did you hear that, bro? She called her *miss*."

I winced as the teacher turned to me, "Factorization."

I blinked. Fractions?

I flipped through the book and couldn't find a chapter called fractions.

"Miss!" I said again, "Can you repeat that."

"Factorization!" the guy named Aarav groaned, "Are you deaf or what?"

I checked the textbook and opened the only chapter that started with an 'F'.

Sahana tapped my back, and I turned around.

"What are you doing?" came the teacher's voice, "Stand up...yes, you!"

I stood.

"Stay like that," she said with an eye roll.

My jaw dropped.

"For the whole period?" I asked, angrily.

"Hmm?" the teacher said, even more furiously, "No! For all my classes from now on."

"Sorry," Sahana muttered.

The door creaked open, and Satya walked in.

"Sorry, Priya ma'am," she said, "I need the girls for a minute."

Satya gestured for us to follow her while Priya glared at me. I followed her out into the hallway, and she pulled out her phone.

She led us to her office where a girl was waiting, but when she saw us, she left. Myna's office used to be really neat before Satya became in charge. But it was never quite as comfy (at least that's what I say to console Satya every time I find a sock in the bookshelf).

A few moments later, a kid, Vijay, walked in with a huge pink grin. Satya groaned. In my opinion, he was really cute, but as far as Satya was concerned, he was there to break stuff and remind her of Myna.

I'm pretty sure Vijay was her brother.

"Vijay!" Satya slammed her fist on the table making the drawer open to reveal another sock, "You ate another Starburst? How many times do I have to hide the packet for you to actually *not* find them?!"

Vijay shrugged with another grin, making me wonder how Satya put up with him.

"I've gotten around five complaints from *five* different rooms," Satya said, opening a complaint record book, "From customers downstairs saying a random kid keeps showing up at their door screaming *Room service*. We've talked about this, Vijay!"

"I didn't do it," Vijay protested, "I swear this time it wasn't me!"

"Then?" Satya asked with a sigh.

If Vijay didn't do it then he probably would have encouraged one of his friends to do it, which was worse.

"It was Aarav Sharma," Vijay said with a chuckle.

Satya groaned, leaning back on her chair. I was pretty sure *I* had an Aarav in my class.

I was also pretty sure Satya had no idea who Aarav Sharma was.

"Which one is Aarav Sharma?" Satya asked, rubbing her temples, confirming my theory.

"The tall one," Vijay said unhelpfully because, as far as I could recall, Aarav was short.

Satya's phone started ringing and I looked down at the caller ID, and gasped.

"Well, tell him not to," Satya said, even more unhelpfully, pushing Vijay away.

He curiously looked at the phone, but Satya blocked it, standing up.

"Hello?" Satya said into the phone nervously, looking at me as Vijay left with what looked like a Starburst packet.

"Satya?" Asked the gravelly voice of Grandsire Bhishma.

Bhishma was one of the big shots in the Mahabharata.

He was also the boss of everyone.

"Yes, sir," Satya asked, sitting down on her chair again.

"Is Ambika there?" He asked.

Oops. I rocked back and forth as Satya hesitated, looking at me.

"No, sir," Satya said slowly.

She should've left it at that.

"She's left us," She added, "We had a disagreement."

There was silence on the other side and another voice whispered something.

"Satya, in that case the message we received is *not* a joke," he said, "Ambika is creating her own army. You're up against a new force, and…Ambika wants the throne of both Hastinapura and Indraprastha too."

Satya put the phone down as the call ended, her eyes wide.

"I'm so sorry," I said, "This is my fault."

"No, it's not," Sahana said, "But seriously? Ambika?"

Satya shrugged, "I know! I can't believe it!"

My mind was racing. I couldn't believe that Ambika would go *that* far, but she had. If she was going to confidently say that she was going to fight, then she would've already started recruiting armies. Either that or she was super confident.

I missed being confident. The last time I'd felt confident was when we'd seen Brahmari and she told us the gods were on our side…

An idea hit me.

"Can we recruit the devas?" I asked curiously.

The group turned to look at me simultaneously.

In Hindu mythology, supernatural beings were split into two sections: Devas and Asuras; The Devas symbolized good and the Asuras, bad. The devas I was referring to were the ones that controlled forces of nature. For example, Indra, the king of devas and ruler of heaven, controlled the sky and *my* grandfather, Vayu, controlled wind and so on.

There were a *lot* of devas.

"Is that even allowed?" Sahana asked.

"There are rules?" I asked incredulously.

"There *are* rules," Satya agreed, "and recruiting the devas doesn't go against any of them. Still, the idea-"

"Who makes sure we follow the rules?" I asked.

She frowned, "Well, it's actually based on integrity. The rules include stuff like no fighting after sundown and only one-on-one combats were allowed meaning that a bunch of people can't attack one person at once."

"Wait," Amrita said, frowning, "Isn't that what happened to Abhimanyu in the OM?"

"What's that?" I asked, frowning.

"Original Mahabharata," Amrita said, rolling her eyes, "Duh. Catch on."

"Yeah," Satya said, nodding her head, "All the good fighters of the Kaurava army ganged up against one teenager. There's really not much anyone could do about it."

I remembered sobbing over it, and *I* wasn't letting that happen to me, although I doubt anyone would cry.

"That means no one implements them and your life basically hangs on the fine thread of your enemy's moral compass," I said incredulously, "How did that *ever* work?"

"It didn't. Every single rule of war was broken in the OM."

I glanced at Amrita with a nervous look. Rohan's idea of righteousness was probably narrow considering the fact he burnt down an entire building for revenge against me being brought to India.

"I don't really like that system," Amrita said, slowly.

"Yeah," Sahana agreed, "In fact it makes me wonder how *any* of the Pandavas survived..."

Satya nodded with raised eyebrows probably marveling how anybody survived past the *first day*, "Too bad there's nothing we can do abou-"

"How about Bhishma doesn't participate in the war?" I said, my face lighting up, "How about he's the war lawyer guy and we go to *him* if anyone breaks the rule and he'll come up with a punishment."

Satya blinked at me, "That-"

"Is a good idea!" Sahana cut in, "We could do that! Who has Bhisma's phone number?"

Satya shrugged, "You know what? Why not? We can totally use that idea, although it sounds like a kindergartener came up with it. It's not like its *war* or anything."

She smiled, turned and walked away to her office. I beamed because I didn't really voice out great ideas often. Thinking about it, I didn't voice out any ideas no matter how many I had.

Satya came back a few minutes later with her phone and a huge smile.

"He was impressed," She said to me, "And he agreed."

Sahana and I shared a high five of joy while Amrita and Shyamala fist bumped.

At least now, we'd die with justice! Oh, the joy…

"Now where were we?" Satya asked, "Something about recruiting someone?"

"How do we get to Indra Loka?" I said with a smile.

ROHAN

HEARTLESS

"Whatever actions are performed by a man under whatever circumstances, he gets the fruits of those actions under whatever circumstances they may be performed." – Lord Krishna, Mahabharata

Duryodhana put his phone down, his mouth still open wide. It'd been that way since he'd started reading a message Bhishma had sent.

"Well?" Bhanumati asked, "What did he say?"

Duryodhana looked at me, "She left them too."

"Ambika?"

He nodded, "She's making her own army. She wants both Hastinapura and Indraprastha."

"What for?" I asked, and Duryodhana shrugged.

I was about to say something when Dhrona, my tutor, came in. He, and my father were the ones who'd trained me my whole life telling me that I was born to rule the kingdom.

"Rohan, you're late," Dhrona said, frustrated.

"Dhrona," Duryodhana called, "Come here one sec."

Dhrona walked to Duryodhana impatiently, "Sir, Rohan's been falling behind. He isn't-"

"You need to start training him as hard as you can," Duryodhana said, looking up, "The hardest you ever have."

I gulped. Dhrona's training was generally harsh. What was he going on about?

"Ambika's forming her own army," Duryodhana continued, "And as hard as it is to believe, she is good at what she does. Rohan needs to be able to do more than fight her now."

The glass Bhanumati was holding shattered on the white cloth as she gasped, "*Duryodhana*!"

"If this leads to war, he needs to," Duryodhana said.

There was no regret in his voice.

He hadn't said it, but the message rang through in bold letters.

He wanted me to kill my sister.

Would he cry about this later? Was he staying strong here for me, or did he genuinely not care?

I stared at him in bewilderment.

Was that how *I* should be? How did he lock his heart away from the world?

How did he have the nerve to tell his son to kill his daughter?

"Rohan," Dhrona commanded.

I shuddered, "Yes, sir."

***

I stared at the maroon stain on my jeans seeping into the denim below it. The grass beneath me was stained too, a reminder of what I'd done.

There, at my feet, lay a rat - a victim to my father's plans, just like me.

It was so small, but now that it was gone, it felt so big. It was a life that I'd taken. Its fur was matted and its eyes that had once looked at me with curiosity were now staring blankly at the sky.

I had killed it.

My trembling hands reached for the blood on my pants, sticky and warm. I wanted, so bad, to get rid of it but every time my fingers neared it, they faltered with disgust at myself.

"Rohan, stand up," Dhrona's voice cut through my sea of guilt like a warship, "Here, kill this one."

Another rat scampered towards me; its whiskers twitched as it sniffed around the dead version of itself.

It looked up at me as I got onto my knees, its nose quivering. Expectant. Waiting for me to end its life too.

"I need a break," I whispered, my voice two octaves lower than it should've bee.

My legs shook, threatening to give away, and I sank deeper into the grass.

Was I a monster, now? Someone who took life so casually?

"You can't handle a rat?" Dhrona lashed at me, "You're destined to be king, Rohan! Weakness is a luxury you can no longer spend time on!"

His words seemed to sting even more than the death of the rat. I *was* weak. I couldn't rule. Especially if it meant doing *this* to humans. To Ambika.

I glared at him, trying to push the blame away, "If you're such an expert at killing, then why don't *you* just do it?"

Dhrona's face seemed to turn to a wrinkly statue, "I'm not fighting Ambika. You are."

I looked away and, once more, my eyes fell on the rat. I rocked back and forth, trying to steady myself. My sword lay by my feet, and I shuddered at the thought of picking it up.

The cold metal was still stained with the blood of its previous victim.

All I had to do was drive the sword through the creature's fragile body.

"Do it!" Dhrona's command echoed around my skull.

I picked up the sword that I'd had since I was ten, but today it felt like I'd never touched it before. It had killed now.

My knuckles turned white as I gripped the hilt, but I wavered.

"I don't need to kill anyone," I chocked, "There *has* to be another way."

Dhrona's laugh was bitter, "Oh, really? What would you do instead?"

"I could maim," I said, averting my gaze from the rat.

"The dead stay silent, boy, but those you maim will come back to haunt you."

The sword trembled in my hands. Maybe I could run away? I wouldn't have to rule this stupid kingdom or kill this stupid rat. I was about to sprint when my father's voice shattered my thoughts.

"Rohan!" His roar echoed across the field, "How is it going? I'm sure you're doing amazing, as always."

Dhrona shifted uncomfortably with disapproval, "Well, sir, he's actually-"

"Shut up, Dhrona," Duryodhana's hand landed on my shoulder with a force that nearly made my knees buckle, "My son can do anything. Go ahead, Rohan. It's just the beginning."

His fingers squeezed me with pride that didn't seem so genuine anymore.

I raised my sword, waiting for the rat to move. Its beady eyes bore into mine. I waited so long it was as if it was mocking me by not running.

The swords hilt was now glazed with sweat.

"I can't."

Duryodhana's expression shifted quickly. It now had no pride or compassion and seemed to be carved in cold, hard steel.

His hand collided against my head with a resonating *smack* making pain scar across my face,

I staggered back.

It hurt today more than it had ever before, but I didn't dare show it.

"You lazy fool!" His voice growled, full of fury, "KILL!"

I shuddered, my fingers closing around the swords hilt once again. I grit my teeth resisting the urge to massage my throbbing jaw.

"Yes, sir."

AMBIKA

POISONED

"Happiness cannot be attained by the weak; it can only be achieved by those who have strength." – Bhishma, Mahabharata

So," Shishir said, kicking the dust on the path we were walking on, "How's life?"

We'd been walking in silence for thirty minutes, and I was *dying* for someone to break it.

By someone, I meant anyone but me.

I shrugged, "Fine."

"Where are we going, again?" Shishir asked, looking at me.

"You'll see," I said, which was the same thing I'd said last time he asked.

Not that our destination was meant to be a surprise, but I felt like if I'd told him, he would convince me not to go. In fact, the whole trip was kind of a surprise to me as well, because it wasn't planned. If I'd thought about it, we would still be back at our little shed near Hastinapura.

"Ambika," Shishir said, crossing his arms, "*Tell* me! I'm getting kind of miffed."

I ignored him, "I sent a note to Bhishma."

That took his attention away from our unknown destination, "Oh! What'd you say?"

"I told him that I was forming my own army and to tell Rohan and Subhadrai to give me the throne. It would make it a lot easier if he listened," I said, nonchalantly.

"Why? You don't want to fight?" Shishir asked.

I did.

"Yeah, but if he'd agreed then we wouldn't have to be *here*," I said, pointing to the hut in front of us.

Shishir's head snapped to the view in front of us. It didn't help that there were bones on the weed-filled ground along with the armor of warriors who came before.

I drew in a sharp breath.

"Hey, Shishir," I said, my voice wavered, "Stay here, okay?"

But it was too late. A lady walked out of the hut. Her eyes met Shishir's, and my heart nearly stopped. I glanced at Shishir who'd turned fifty shades paler.

"You brought us to the *Vishakanyas*?" Shishir asked, his voice strained.

The Vishakanyas were a group of a few select women who were fed poison from a young age. Many hadn't survived, but those who did became one with the poison and could kill with touch.

They were *literally* drop-dead gorgeous.

The woman stepped closer towards us onto the barren land before the hut. I could hear Shishir hyperventilating behind me. Even I was having trouble breathing.

"What brings you here?" the lady drawled, her fingers tracing across the rickety fence around the house.

I couldn't find my voice. My heart was pounding against my chest like a funeral drum.

"Well?" the woman repeated, "Not many people enter willingly."

She pointed at the border behind us that we'd foolishly crossed. I felt a groan build up in my throat. The Vishakanyas were banned from crossing the border!

"Shishir," I whispered, "Cross the line, get out of here."

I stepped back expecting him to do the same, but I bumped into him.

"Move," I hissed.

I glanced at him, trying to get him to budge, but Shishir was frozen in fear.

I gave him a push as the Vishakanya snickered.

I turned to look at her, and gasped. There were now three of them standing right in front of me.

The first one stretched her hand towards me, making me shriek. I scampered behind Shishir trying to pull him back.

I snapped, "Shishir, run!"

He stared at the three ladies in front of him, unmoving. As they stepped towards him, he stumbled back as if awakening from a nightmare. I grabbed the opportunity and dragged him further.

Shishir fell to the ground with a thud, stopping himself with his elbows. He scrambled back with a whimper. The ladies were still slowly walking towards us in coordination as if this had happened before.

I grabbed Shishir's arm, making his head crash on the rock below him. I cried out in fright as the Vishakanyas kneeled before Shishir's still body.

I pulled desperately and he was almost out until the first lady's finger dragged across his calf. I felt Shishir shiver as he crossed the border.

I gasped and stood up as Shishir turned a pale shade of green. I looked up at the lady who squinted at me angrily.

"What brings you here?" the lady repeated.

"I-I need your help." I stuttered, staring at Shishir in shock.

"He is gone," one of the ladies said.

The first one shot her a glare and turned to me, "What would you like us to do?"

"I need to…I have to fight in a war," I gasped, bending down next to Shishir, "I wanted you to be on our side."

She frowned, "You did not come to destroy us?"

I shook my head. I glanced at Shishir wondering if I could touch him.

"Come in," the lady said.

I looked at her apprehensively.

"We have a cure," she said, softly.

I turned to Shishir helplessly, "Um…"

"Come," she persisted.

I stood up to face her. I wanted to believe her.

Shishir *couldn't* be gone. I'd already sent Bhishma the message. Shishir was the only person I had on my side. He was also the only friend I had anymore. I took a step past the boundary and expected her to poison me too.

But she turned away and walked into the hut. I felt the eyes of the other two on me, but I didn't move.

In a minute the Vishakanya returned and placed a dark vial at my feet.

I took it slowly, and smiled, "Well, I still have that position in my army if you want."

They looked at each other with suspicion.

I took a deep breath, "If it helps, I can take your poison away."

They glanced at me intrigued.

"There's a flower in the palace garden," I said, "My mother told me that it's so powerful it can even remove poison from the veins of a Vishakanya."

They looked at me, full of excitement.

"But to get the flower, I need to be the queen of the kingdom," I explained, "It's extremely guarded."

"We agree to help you," the first Vishakanya said, "But first you might want to heal your friend."

I glanced at Shishir and nodded.
"Thank you."

AMBIKA

I SING FOR INVISIBLE INSTRUMENTS

"The weak cannot forgive; the strong can, forgiveness is an attribute of the strong." – Krishna, Mahabharata

Put a sock in it,' Shishir said, obviously annoyed with me, "I nearly died."

"You shut up" I said, quite happy with myself, "I recruited the *Vishakanyas*! Rohan can kiss the throne goodbye."

"You do realize that a thousand poison ladies aren't enough?" Shishir asked, "You've got to get at least one more army if you want to stay alive for *one* day."

"Well then, Mister I-know-everything-you-don't, do you have any suggestions?" I said turning to him, sternly.

Shishir wasn't looking sound even after being healed. He was still pretty weak and yesterday he'd even *lost* to me while we were dueling.

That's saying a lot, because Shishir's pretty talented, and he *taught* me how to swordfight.

Shishir looked around the forest we'd decided to take refuge in, "Did you know that this is the forest the Pandavas went to while in exile?"

I looked at him in confusion, "So?"

"While they were here, the Kauravas wanted to flex that they were living a happier life than the Pandavas and came to the forest. While they were here your mom, dad, your brother and sister got captured by the Gandharva king, Chitrasena,' Shishir continued, 'By your brother and sister, I mean Duryodhana's kids in the OM, Lakshman and Lakshmanaa."

I nodded, "I know who my siblings are. What's a Gandharva, again?"

"They're celestial beings who are known for their musical talent. Anyways, Yudhishthira found out what had happened and sent Arjuna to help your dad. Arjuna fought with Chitrasena and killed a million Gandharvas and released your dad. The Gandharva king was pretty impressed, but if we're lucky he might have some lingering feelings of resentment."

I got what he was trying to imply, "You want to recruit a bunch of singers?"

"They're obviously talented, because your dad's no slacker," Shishir said.

"My dad's a slacker when his ego is clouding his sense," I said, "And that's obviously what was happening."

"Listen," Shishir said, "The devas won't help us. The asuras won't help us, but the Gandharvas are closely knit with human happenings. They know about the war for sure, and they'll also be wanting a part in it. They're not as powerful as the devas, but we'll definitely have a plus side. While my uncle, Balarama, was traveling around here, he found a few Gandharva kingdoms. I know for a fact that one is in this forest. If we recruit Gandharvas and their 'cousins', the Yakshas, we'll probably have a good chance in the war against Rohan and Subhadrai. I don't know about Subhadrai, but Rohan's not bad at what he does."

I still wasn't sure about the Gandharva's, but I knew that the Yaksha's were good at fighting.

"It normally takes me a few days to start thinking straight after being sick," I said with a smile, "Good job."

He smiled back, "So, are we giving it a try?"

"We could do worse," I decided.

Shishir got up from the foot of the tree he was leaning on, "I don't really know where the kingdom is, but if we find a clearing and do something to impress the Gandharvas, *they* might find us."

It didn't take us long to find a clearing, but I didn't get what Shishir meant by "impressing the Gandharvas" so, I asked him.

"Can you sing?" He asked, "I know you're rubbish at dance, but I reckon you've still got a pretty good voice."

I froze, almost as still as Shishir when he'd seen the Vishakanyas.

"You want me to sing?" I asked in shock, "Well, what will *you* do? The Gandharvas *are* mainly guys. They might be more impressed if a guy sang."

"Nah, they'll be more impressed if you sang."

I looked at him, lost. I honestly had no problem singing, but I didn't want to do it in front of him *and* a bunch of celestial beings.

"How about we both sing?" I asked.

Shishir's face went blank as if he hadn't expected that.

He looked at me hesitantly, "In that case, what are we singing?"

I frowned, "Something Carnatic, probably."

Carnatic music was Indian classical music.

"Wow," he said, "Something Carnatic. You obviously don't realize how many Carnatic songs there are, do you?"

"I don't know," I said, panic entering my voice for absolutely no reason, "What should we sing?"

"It should be something fast and upbeat," Shishir said, "D'you remember *Kalinga Narthana Thillana*?"

I raised my eyebrows at him. Of *course*, I knew Kalinga Narthana Thillana. He taught me *that* too, along with all the other Carnatic songs I knew.

"I'll take that as a yes," he said.

He sat down on the grass, crisscross-applesauce, and gestured for me to sit down beside him.

When I did, I realized how scared I was. What if the Gandharvas didn't like it? Or what if they liked it and asked for another one? What if they noticed who my dad was and without asking any questions, killed me?

Shishir started singing and pulled me out of my mental breakdown.

It was sudden. It was fast. It was exactly what I needed.

He beamed at me as he sang and gestured for me to join. So, I did. One word after the other, and it all came back to me. I might have even laughed. It'd been so long since Shishir and I had sung together. The last time we did *this* song was with Nisata. The memory would've brought a tear to my eye, but today was different.

Today I was singing again, so I smiled.

We were five minutes into the song when a drum started playing to accompany us. I was about to scream, but Shishir gestured for me to keep singing. Then a violin. I heard Shishir laugh in delight as I sang my solo.

That's when a frightful thought struck me. In two more minutes was Nisata's solo. Shishir must have remembered at the same time because we both glanced at each other fearfully and when it came, we froze. Almost at once the instruments stopped.

We waited in silence for three more seconds, then there was a large thud, and I felt a bag being thrown over my head.

SUBHADRAI

GODLY GRANDPAS RULE

"The mind is everything. What you think, you become." – Lord Krishna, Bhagavad Gita

There's no right time for family to show up. They're always welcome. That is, except when you're about to go to the devas to recruit them into your tiny army. In that case, it's best that your obnoxious, teenage cousin brothers don't show up.

So obviously, out of all the times you would need them, that's when they show up with their spirits high and maturity low.

The five of us were about to light-travel into Indra Loka when a flash of light which was not created by us appeared and with it the sons of the Pandavas.

"What's up?" said Shrutakarma with a wave, "Where are you guys going?"

The five of us went still and I gasped in shock.

"Hey guys!" Satya said, slowly and carefully, "This is unexpected."

"No, it's not," Prathivindhya said, "We told you when we went for the cricket match last week, we'd come to help you prepare for war. How many kingdoms have you got?"

The question was directed to me. I gulped.

"Two and a half," I said, "If you count Ayodhya."

At least we were honest. Along with those two kingdoms, we also had a bunch of bugs and snakes. I mentioned that.

"I *told* you we should've come earlier," Shrutakarma said.

Yeah, our brothers were proud feminists.

"We're actually on our way to recruit someone," Satya said, "So, you guys can kick back and relax."

"If Yudhishthira told Bhima to kick back and relax, the Kauravas would have won the war," Sutasoma said, "You don't waste good allies like that."

"Alright, then go recruit a few kingdoms, I don't care," Satya said, impatiently and with another flash of light, we were gone.

"That was unexpected," I whispered, as we hit the ground once more.

"Yeah," Sahana agreed, "They should have called before they left."

"Not that," I said, looking behind her.

She turned around and gasped. Behind us was a bustling community in the sky filled with people wearing tall conical crowns adorned with jewels, laughing, and walking around happily. At the center of it was a large white palace with a large white elephant before it and a ginormous green tree. There were lakes of something that looked like butter and honey. There was also a long stream of offerings to the gods, vehicles zooming around, and amidst the flying chariots there were also a few Mercedes and Ferraris.

There was no sun nor moon there, since Surya (the god of the sun) and Chandra (the god of the moon) lived here they didn't work in Indra Loka. It was... glowing itself.

We started to walk towards the palace and noticed sages walking down the streets. Riding around in the expensive cars were people who Satya told me were heroes who'd died in battle.

There weren't many of them though because most of them had been reborn back on Earth. The closer we got to the palace; the less ordinary residents seemed. The heroes with their fancy cars were replaced by gorgeous women and men who were walking around, belting out songs at the drop of the hat, holding musical instruments. They were the Gandharvas. There were also few young ladies who were floating in and out of the palace as if they were dancing. Satya said that they were *apsaras*, the court musicians of Indra.

"We're at Amaravati," Satya said cheerfully, "The capital of heaven, and home of Indra.'

We walked past the apsaras and towards the elephant.

"That's Airavata," Satya said, "He's Indra's elephant. He guards the palace."

She went over to the elephant to ask for permission to enter and told us to wait there.

I turned to Shyamala, "This place is cool."

She nodded in agreement, "I honestly did expect more *apsaras* here though."

Satya gestured for us to enter the palace and we walked past Airavata who trumpeted positively, so I guess he wouldn't kill us.

As we walked past the gate, we entered the gardens of Nandana marked by a golden plaque. It was filled with a lot more *apsaras* than there were outside the palace which seemed to clear Shyamala's doubt. There were plenty of exotic-looking trees. Especially one huge tree in the middle that seemed to glow quite a bit more than everything else that was there.

"Have you been here before?" I asked Satya because she seemed like she knew the place.

"Yeah, I came here to get Vishwakarma to build the new Hotel K for me after Rohan burnt the first one," Satya revealed, "And if you thought all this was cool, wait till you see the palace."

I didn't have to wait for long. We entered the palace after a five-minute walk past the gardens.

I went in after everyone else, and was, hence, the last to be blown away. Indra's main hall was LEGENDARY!!!

"Oh, my goodness," Sahana whispered, "Can you *believe* my dad lived here for a while?"

I shook my head in disbelief.

It was true. While all his brothers were suffering down in the forest, Arjuna came up to heaven for a while. I've always wondered why he didn't take all the Pandavas with him.

But nobody's perfect. (Later I would find out that Arjuna did not go to heaven for a pleasure vacation, but to hone his weaponry skills with his father and to get a shiny new bow. During his visit he was also cursed, so I guess his life wasn't totally chill.)

"Well, your grandfather is the king of this place, so the fact that your father stayed here for a while isn't that big of a deal," Shyamala pointed out.

At the center of the hall was a row of thrones, (one for each of the important devas, I suppose), and smack in the middle was a huge throne where Indra and his wife Sachi were seated.

We went over to them and bowed.

"What is it you want?" Indra asked, sipping from his goblet of nectar, "Is the hotel in ashes again?"

"No, sir," Satya said, her head bowed, "We came to ask for a favor."

This caught the other devas' interest, because it wasn't everyday five girls came to Indra Loka for a favor.

"Yes?" Indra asked, taking another suspicious sip.

"Sir, I'm sure you are aware of the war that is occurring on Earth," Satya said.

"Yes, yes," Indra said, "What about it?"

"We were hoping for, um, support from the devas?" Satya asked, lifting her head a bit.

There was a beat of silence.

"I'm sorry," Indra sighed, "I can't do that."

Satya was about to leave, but I didn't want to go back and have the boys shove more insults in our faces.

"Sir, please" Sahana said, "We could really use the help!"

He looked at her, "Who are you?"

"I'm Sahana," she said, "Daughter of Arjuna."

His eyes immediately lit up, "Sahana! You know I've met Shrutakarma, but I personally wanted to have met you instead. Arjuna obviously hasn't spoken much about you, because the last time we met was before you were born, but I certainly have heard quite a lot."

I looked at Sahana who looked as if she didn't know how to react to that.

"You know what? This isn't how I expected my first meeting with you would go," Indra said, "I was actually expecting to give you a gift like any other grandfather… I can't really give you the *devas*, because believe it or not we *do* have jobs. If we all came down to help you, then the sun wouldn't rise or set, the world would be depleted of air and water, and a few farmers would miss their crop."

Sahana looked at me, "I'd never thought of that."

"Most never do," Indra laughed, "But I've got a duty, and I must keep doing it. Although I could give you the Maruts. They *have* been asking me for a holiday. I think this is quite a good one, don't you think so?"

Sahana glanced at Satya frantically, *who are the Maruts?*

"Say yes," she whispered.

Sahana nodded enthusiastically, "Yeah, for sure."

"Well then, that's that. The Maruts will be sent to you during the war. Fear not!" Indra laughed, "And feel free to take a few weapons from my weaponry, girls. I'll take you there myself."

He seemed more like a grandfather than the king of the devas now. He cheerily led us to the weaponry.

"Consider yourself lucky," He said, "Most people have to go through a lot of meditation for this, including your father. To have me give it to you… well, it's quite a privilege, if I do say so myself."

He opened two large golden doors and led us to a ginormous room decked with beautiful weapons and chariots. At once Satya walked over to a spear and a war chariot at the corner of the room.

"That was your father's," Indra said, proudly, "And you can have it too if you'd like."

Satya thanked the king and boarded the chariot with a grin.

I didn't focus on her for long because a large, beautiful bow caught my eye (never in my existence would I have expected myself to call a bow beautiful). Sahana walked over to it in awe. Indra didn't say anything, so she grasped it cautiously.

Sahana picked it up from the table it was on and looked at it in awe.

"The Gandiva," she gasped, plucking the string.

The sound was so deafening that Satya dropped her spear onto my head.

"Ah!" I screamed, rubbing my head, "Watch it."

"I don't think I can argue about you not having that," Indra smiled, "Your father will be *extremely* proud. And along with this I'll give you a few special arrows too. I'll explain each one to you later, but they'll definitely be of use to you."

Sahana nodded in thanks and walked over to me. I turned around and realized I was standing in front of a mace.

"That was my dad's," I noticed, pointing at the label that stated so, "But I don't really want a mace…"

I'd never progressed past the sword during training. I stared at the mace in envy.

Amrita walked over, "Hey, Subhadrai. Are you going to take that, or…?"

I shook my head slowly, "No, I don't think so."

Amrita immediately grabbed it with joy, "So I can, have it?"

"Yeah, why not?" I laughed.

I walked over to the swords section and picked one up.

"Ah," Indra said, "That sword's name is Asi. It *did* belong to Nakula for a while, though it belonged to many other people too."

"I guess my name's on that list,' I said, holding the hilt firmly.

I twirled it around and noticed the lion staring into my soul with an expression that was meant to be justice. It was just like the one I'd used during training.

"Can I take this?" Shyamala said, lifting a huge sword.

Indra nodded with consent.

Shyamala frowned at the label, "It says that it's my father's."

"I thought Sahadeva used an ax," I asked.

I nodded in agreement.

"Ah well, you can't trust everything you see on TV," Indra shrugged, "Come Sahana. I'll show you the arrows. The rest of you can explore the garden."

ROHAN

WHAT HAD I DONE?

Sorrow comes after happiness and happiness after sorrow. One does not always suffer sorrow not always enjoy happiness – Veda Vyasa, Mahabharata

I'm sorry," Bhanumati said.

I whirled around looking at the figure of my mother standing in the doorway, "Huh?"

"I'm so sorry, Rohan," she said, coming over to me, "I haven't been talking to you much. I know that training's been hard."

"Oh," I said, shrugging, "It's okay."

It wasn't like I could tell her otherwise.

"No, Rohan, it isn't," she said, "I *genuinely* think that you can be king. I'm not favoring you over Ambika, and I want you to know that I will never do that either, but you, like your father says, are the only one ready for the throne."

"Wow, really encouraging. I've never heard *that* before."

"No, Rohan. I mean the *throne*. Ambika and Subhadrai are training themselves for war, but you've gone further than that. Don't feel bad that Subhadrai has gotten better at recruiting armies than she was two weeks ago. Even if she sat on the throne, she wouldn't be able to do more than sit. She cannot rule, Rohan. Not as well as you can."

"How would you know that?"

"Because I see you do it, Rohan," she put her hand on my cheek with a sad smile, "Every day."

She really believed that.

My father and Dhrona thought so too.

So why shouldn't I rule?

I placed my hand on my mother's, "I'll win, Ma. Don't worry."

She took her hand off my cheek and stepped back, "I'm not worrying."

When she left, I fell back on my bed heaving a long sigh.

I really *was* going to win. If not for me, then for her.

***

"Faster!" Dhrona screamed.

231

I raced towards the end of the huge field trying to catch the horse that he'd sent galloping away.

"If your horse runs away in the middle of war, are you just going to let yourself be stranded, boy?"

I picked up my speed, but just as I was about to grab the reins, Advaith stood in front of me.

I halted, crashing onto him, falling down.

"Bro!" I yelled, spitting sand out of my mouth, "What do you want?"

"Ambika's making her own army?" he asked, bewildered.

Had this guy been living under a rock or something for the past week? As if I needed a reminder. At least now Subhadrai knew what it was like to lose her greatest ally.

"I had no idea," I muttered, rolling my eyes.

"ROHAN!" Dhrona scolded, striding towards me, "Did I ask you to stop?"

"No, sir," I sighed, pushing myself up, "Sorry."

Dhrona looked at Advaith, "Who told you to come here?"

He turned pale, "Sorry, sir."

"Advaith, get lost," Dhrona snapped, "and, Rohan, run a hundred laps."

I groaned, falling back down, "Advaith!"

"Sorry," He repeated, "But, seriously Rohan, are you going to kill her?"

I shrugged, "I don't know. Don't ask me! I can't even kill a rat!"

"When did you try killing a rat?" Advaith asked, furrowing his brows.

"Don't ask," I said, stretching my feet out on the sandy ground, "It's not like *you* can kill."

"I can maim," Advaith said, sounding a lot like me.

"Oh really?" I asked, "Then why don't you?"

Advaith looked at me aghast, "You want me to maim your sister?"

I shrugged, "Why not?"

He couldn't do it. Advaith was a coward.

"Okay," he said, "I will."

"Wait, wha-"

But by the time I'd gotten up to stop him, he'd disappeared.

I stared at the place where Advaith was standing a moment ago.

What had I done?

SUBHADRAI

THIS IS TRASH

"The greatest enemy is the one within." – Lord Krishna, Bhagavad Gita

There's an arrow that shoot's out snakes!" Sahana gushed, "And another one that makes everyone on the battlefield fall asleep, although he *did* tell me not to use that one… I'm totally using that one."

Indra had given Sahana a whole bunch of arrows and a quiver big enough to hold them. The five of us came out of Indra Loka without any of our weapons, though. We were promised that they would be delivered to our hotel by the time we reached it.

And (as Satya had later told us when we were in the garden), the Maruts were aggressive storm-gods who would totally help us kick some butt.

When we reached the hotel, we found our weapons in the lobby and Tara, the stable-keeper, told us our chariots were safely parked outside with the weapons.

We trudged up and found the PS in Satya's office laughing about something.

"So?" Prathivindhya asked, "Who'd you recruit?"

"Sixty storm gods and a bunch of cool weapons," Sahana said, "You?"

Shrutakarma shot a smirk at Sutasoma who gave us a big grin.

"I thought you'd never ask," he said, proudly, "We formally got three *akshauhinis* from Panchalam, Draupadi's kingdom, even though I'm pretty sure she wouldn't have given one to the Kauravas anyways. An *akshauhini* consists of twenty-one thousand, eight hundred seventy chariots, twenty-one thousand, eight hundred seventy elephants, sixty-five thousand six hundred ten horsemen, one hundred nine thousand, three hundred fifty-foot soldiers, by the way. I remember *that* because my dad made me memorize it for a lifetime supply of Jolly Ranchers. Then, we got another *akshauhini* from Matsya because Abhimanyu is engaged to the princess of Matsya."

I wonder if he had gotten those Jolly Ranchers and if he was allowed to share.

"Then there are princes from our cricket team," Shrutakarma continued, 'one *akshauhini* from the kingdom of Dasarna, Cholas, Anarta, Kekeya each. Then half an *akshauhini* from Dwaraka provided by Abhimanyu, *and* from our cousin, Bhima's son with the princess of rakshasas (demons), Ghatotkacha we got one *akshauhini* of demons."

Stunned silence.

I HAD A DEMON BROTHER?! AWESOME!

"You're welcome," Prativindhya added.

I hugged Sutasoma as I squealed, "OH MY GODS! YOU GUYS ARE THE BEST!"

Prathivindhya gave Satya a smile, Shyamala and Amrita fist bumped Satanika and Shrutasena, and Shrutakarma ignored Sahana.

"But what you guys did was impressive too," Sutasoma shrugged.

"Yeah," Sahana agreed, "Guess who owns the Gandiva now?"

Shrutakarma jaw dropped in shock, "THAT'S NOT FAIR!"

"Deal with it, loser," Sahana said, sticking her tongue out at him.

There was a knock at the door and a girl peeped her head in, "Satya, Asmi ma'am wants the American girls to come. She wants them to act in the annual day play."

Satya grinned, "Yeah sure, Saranya. Take them *and* the boys."

She rubbed her hand gleefully.

"Asmi ma'am is *amazing* at scripts," she said, with a devilish laugh, "That's a lie, by the way."

***

I stared at the script once more in shock.

"How did this lady ever get a job?" I wondered aloud.

Amrita rubbed her temples, "When I stab the hero in the back, should I *actually* laugh or do the 'BWA-HA-HA-HA' in the script?"

"Beats me," Sahana laughed, "But it'd be funnier if you follow the script."

Sutasoma walked in laughing, "I didn't realize this was a comedy!"

"It's not," I said, with a sigh, "I asked her. It's an action-suspense."

Sutasoma looked back at the paper in confusion.

"This," Prathivindhya said, "is trash. I'm saying this as a son of Yudhishthira who is bound to tell the truth."

The drama teacher then walked in with a sigh, "Okay, places everybody! The guests are here!"

"Wait, we're doing this in front of an audience?" I asked, horrified.

The drama teacher, Asmi Gupta, looked at me in disgust, "And you're supposed to be queen. Ugh."

I couldn't tell if she meant in the play or in real life, but I think she was talking about the latter. I looked at Sahana.

"Is it wrong for me to *not* want to do this in public?"

She looked at the script, "No, not. At. All."

We walked out onto the large stage, and I saw Satya in the front row with a huge smile. She sat next to Abhimanyu and his fiancé, Uttarai.

"How old is Abhimanyu?" I asked Shrutakarma.

He frowned, "Twenty-seven, I guess."

I raised my eyebrows, "He is the most childish adult I've met in my entire life."

"Curtains," the Asmi ma'am called out loudly.

I looked at the script once more. *I* was supposed to be the hero. I took a deep breath as the spotlight landed on me.

I turned to Amrita, who was the friend/traitor, "Come friend," I said, "We shall go to the king's palace and pay our respects to him!"

Amrita nodded, *'Yes'* she turned to the audience and tried to do a malicious grin, "Haha. I am so evil."

There were a few snickers from the audience and Amrita lost her 'evil-villain' posture trying to contain her laughter.

Shyamala and Sahana ran onto stage in small straw hats that were supposed to represent that they were villagers. They looked as if they regretted ever finding out that they were KOMC.

They said in unison, "Oh brave warrior, do not go see the king. He is pretty angry."

"Nonsense!" Amrita said, grabbing my hand, "We shall go now."

"Suit yourselves," Sahana and Shyamala said as they left the stage and Prathivindhya walked in wearing a paper crown.

"Why are you here?" he thundered.

Amrita did another evil grin, nearly making me fall on the floor in fits of laughter, "We have come to pay our respects to you."

She drew her floppy, aluminum sword and pretended to stab Prathivindhya.

I glanced at the audience in time to see Satya leave the auditorium talking to someone on the phone.

Amrita then turned to me, and then pretended to stab me in the back, "I AM SO SMART! BWAHAHAHA!"

I heard snorts and giggles from the audience.

As I fell onto the floor, Sutasoma walked in, "Fear not! I shall kill this backstabbing traitor who literally backstabs!"

He then proceeded to pretend-punch Amrita in the face causing her death. Then Satanika and Shrutasena walked in dragging a huge cardboard box with Shrutakarma sitting on the top, covered in gray, grinning in satisfaction.

"I am a rock," he said, in between laughter, "No one can live!"

With that Shrutakarma jumped off the box onto Sutasoma and the curtains closed.

I heard deafening applause coming from the other end.

"I never knew that applause could convey sarcasm," Amrita muttered, as she got up, dusting herself off.

The only one who even *remotely* enjoyed their role was Shrutakarma.

"Forget becoming Shah Rukh Khan, I'm never stepping on stage again," Prativindhya said, rolling his eyes, as he left the stage.

"Satya left the audience," I said, worried, "She seemed pretty excited to see us perform. I wonder what happened."

Sahana shrugged, "Well, at least there's one person who won't tease us about what happened."

"Nah, Abhimanyu was recording it," Amrita said, "We're doomed."

That's when Satya ran in, brandishing a letter in her hand, "Subhadrai, come with me."

I glanced at Sahana who shrugged, then followed Satya trying to calm my mini panic-attack. I'd grown to dislike letters after all the recent incidents involving them (I'm looking at you, Ambika).

"Subhadrai, Bhishma wants to meet the three of you on Wednesday," she said, quickly, "He said that they're going to discuss whether or not a war is really needed. He said that by the time the meeting happened, we should be prepared for war, because if the decision of war is made, then there will be no time to prepare after that."

She looked at me to make sure I understood, which I did. I nodded to show it. I tried to put all my remaining confidence in that nod. I wanted her to see that I was ready to win. That. War.

We had quite a few kingdoms. With the princes' random cricket connections, we could get up to eleven, which was enough.

Although, a tiny part of me hoped that we wouldn't have to deal with the whole war at all.

"Subhadrai," Satya said, as I was leaving, "Bring the girls to my office. We need to talk."

****

"What do you mean the chariots are missing?" I asked, in shock.

"It was Ambika," Satya said, with a sigh, "She left a note."

She handed me a small piece of paper and on it was small crisp writing that said: *Thanks for the gift. I'll be keeping it at MY kingdom.*

"What does *that* mean?" I asked, confused.

"I suppose she's talking about Hastinapura."

I looked once more at the "MY" on the letter. She seemed pretty confident.

"Has Ambika even recruited any armies?" Sahana asked.

Satya nodded, "One. She's gotten one akshauhini from Dwaraka."

"Didn't we have the Dwaraka kingdom?" I asked.

"We got one and a half akshauhinis,' Satya said, 'She took another one. If we recruit a kingdom, it doesn't mean we get the whole army."

"Who was that boy with her that day?" I asked, "He looked a lot like Abhimanyu."

Satya looked at me hesitantly, "Well, there are two possibilities. Ambika has two friends: Nisata and Shishir. *Both* of them look like Abhimanyu. They're all cousins."

Now that I'd met him, it was hard to believe that Nisata would be scheming with Ambika. I didn't recognize the other name.

"Which one was it?" I asked.

"It wasn't Nisata," Satya said, confidently, "From what you said, it seems like Nisata is on our side. I don't know

Shishir well, but I know that if there's one thing, he had in common with Ambika it's that he's stubborn."

I nodded, not knowing what to do with that information.

AMBIKA

MY FAULT

"Your own self is your best friend, and your own self is your worst enemy." – Lord Krishna, Bhagavad Gita

I grasped around the dark room looking for Shishir. I tried to talk, but I didn't hear anything when I did.

Finally, my hand caught on something, and I grabbed it hoping it was Shishir's hand. The second my fingers wrapped around the hand, the light came back on and to my relief it *was* Shishir.

I let go of his hand, "Where are we?"

He looked around, running his hands through his hair in thought, "I have *no* idea."

There was a white room with intricate golden engravings on the wall that looked like musical instruments. At the center of the wall behind us was a golden door with a *veena* (an Indian instrument) engraved on it.

As soon as we looked at it, it swung open revealing a man with a tall pointy crown. He held Shishir's sword in one hand and in the other hand, mine.

"Daughter of Duryodhana," he said, glancing at me, "Son of Krishna. What a surprise."

I glanced at Shishir and mouthed *I think it's the Gandharva king.*

"Ha!" the king said, happily, "It *is* the Gandharva king! I'm King Chitrasena."

He smiled happily and handed me my sword.

I took it and bowed, grateful that Shishir did the same.

"Your majesty, I said, taking a deep breath, "I need your help."

"I know, I heard your conversation, Chitrasena said, with a smile, "Your singing was gorgeous."

I felt a forest fire of happiness light in my heart leading me to say, "So, you'll join us?"

Shishir sucked in a breath behind me, and I assumed he thought my question was too straightforward.

Chitrasena did not seem to think so, "Of course! You want me to join your side of the army for your war against Prince Rohan and Princess Subhadrai! I love this idea! I don't like the Pandavas *or* the Kauravas and look at you! You come here looking to fight both of them! Of *course* I'll say yes! And

I'll ask the boss, Lord Kubera, if we can take the Yakshas too. Don't you worr– Are you okay?"

The question was directed to Shishir. I turned to look at him and saw that his knees had buckled, and he'd gone pale again.

"Yeah, yeah," he said, grabbing my shoulder for support and straightening up again.

I felt my forest fire go out with a wave of guilt. I'd gotten Shishir into this…

"Ahh," Chitrasena said, "You went to the Vishakanyas, huh? Their *anti-venom* needs an anti-venom. It's *so* useless. Come on, boy."

He slapped Shishir's back, playfully and led him to the exit.

Then he turned to me, "By the way, I've transported Subhadrai's team's chariots to Hastinapura. That should slow them down for a while."

I smiled gratefully.

"I even made it seem like *you* did it," Chitrasena called back as he left the room with Shishir.

Shishir gasped in pain and the king hurried away a bit quicker leaving me alone in the empty room hoping that Shishir would heal quickly. That's when another Gandharva came into the room and handed me a note.

"From the grandsire, Bhishma," he said in a low, gruff voice, then left.

I took the paper and unfolded it to see in Bhishma's familiar handwriting, a note in Sanskrit. I quickly read it, my eyes widening.

I hoped we were ready for war because it was far sooner than we thought.

***

Shishir was back on his feet the next week, but was still a bit weaker than he was before the Vishakanya. He still couldn't pin me to the floor while we were fencing, and he was killing himself about it.

"Maybe *I* got better," I said, trying to cheer him up as he sat under a tree grumpily.

"You *did*, but still!" Shishir groaned, "You're not even *trying* your best! I can't believe this. Bhishma said we might have the war on Wednesday, and I'm weaker than Nisata all of a sudden!"

I laughed. Even when the poor guy wasn't there, Shishir would find a way to insult him.

"You're not," I said, still smiling, "I don't think anyone can stoop that low. You need to practice. Wednesday is far away, right?"

"It's Monday," Shishir said, with a grunt.

He looked up at me, worried, and I returned the look. Time had gone by so quickly.

"I don't think our army is big enough," Shishir said, "One akshauhini of humans, about a thousand poisonous ladies and a few more thousand divine beings that can play any instrument in the world. I don't know… it doesn't feel like enough. Even the Vishakanyas can't use their powers randomly, according to the laws Bhishma sent us. They can only use their poison for self-defense. Or else, they'll also have to fight."

I was *not* aware of that.

"They can't?" I asked, shocked.

Shishir shook his head no.

I didn't feel confident anymore either.

"Wow," I rolled my eyes, "It would have been helpful if you mentioned that, I don't know, *before* we recruited them."

Shishir glared at me, "I was dead. Literally."

I opened my mouth, and it stayed like that for a while, "Alright, fine. So, you want to recruit one more *akshauhini*?"

He nodded.

"Alright then" I said, with a sigh, "Who?"

"Anish."

I stared at him, "Who?"

He didn't say anything and looked back at me for a second.

"Oh," I said, quietly, "No. Nonononono. No way!"

"Stop saying that," Shishir said, "He's not that bad anymore! Plus, you were in *second grade* when you got angry at him. Do you really think you can still trust *those* emotions?"

I did. Second grade emotions were the only ones that made sense.

"Listen, genius," I said, putting my hands on my hips, 'I would rather recruit my *brother* than this guy."

"Ambika, he has a huge army. They're good too!"

"I said no."

"Do you even remember why the two of you fought?"

I focused really hard on the blade of grass under Shishir's shoes.

"Ambika!" Shishir whined, "*Please*. We'll get a horse from the Gandharvas and ride to the kingdom of Chedi. He won't say no."

"I won't say yes," I said, stomping my foot on the ground, "I cried nonstop for *seven* days. Even if I don't remember what he did, it *had* to suck!"

"I *know*," Shishir said, trying to be as sympathetic as possible, "And *I* was the one who calmed you down. *I* was the one who told you that he was a nobody and that you should ignore him. So, if *I'm* the one telling you to go recruit him, it's for a good reason."

I examined his expression carefully. Under his pale skin and tussled hair, he really seemed like he believed what he was saying.

I'd nearly killed him

The least I could do was listen.

"Fine," I said, "*You* can go recruit him, but I'm not coming."

His face broke into a thank-you smile, "You're the best."

SUBHADRAI

THE MOON FORMATION

"The mind is its own place, and in itself can make a heaven of hell, a hell of heaven." – Lord Krishna, Bhagavad Gita

I can't believe we're doing this," I said, sitting down at the table, "I bet *nobody* in all of history has binge watched ten movies and went out for dinner two days before starting a war."

"I bet it's happened," Sahana said, rubbing her eyes in exhaustion, "Plus, you don't even know if you'll get into a war."

"What else could he *possibly* do?" Amrita asked, tightening her ponytail as she checked the menu.

"Rock, Paper, Scissors," Shyamala said, as serious as those three words could sound.

Satya laughed, "I'm pretty sure that one way or the other, this thing is going to end in war."

I shrugged, "Whatever it is, my mom is going to kill me for having watched TV that long."

"Not if Rohan does it first," Shrutakarma said, with a smirk.

"*Shrutakarma*!" Prathivindhya said, looking at his brother angrily, "Don't say that."

The son of Arjuna smiled, and tried to grab one of Sutasoma's five dosas which were a lot larger than the ones my mom made back in California. They didn't even fit the plate they were on! Once, I'd seen my dad eat two of those, but five was a new record. I also think he was going to ask for more.

"You better stop eating if you want to fight in the war," Satanika said, punching Sutasoma's arm as he grabbed a samosa on Prathivindhya's plate.

"You shut up," Sutasoma said, "At least I'm *eating*."

The son of Nakula had hardly eaten half his dosa before giving up. That's how huge it was.

"Subhadrai," Amrita said, poking me, and pointing at a group of three in front of us, "Look!"

I glanced at the table she was pointing at and saw three kids sitting at the table.

"I don't really care how you feel. Are you in or not?" asked the girl sitting at the table.

One of the boys scratched his head nervously while the other looked at him expectantly.

"Yeah, I'm in. But why won't you get over it?" the boy asked.

"Oh, my gods," I whispered in shock, "It's Ambika."

At once, everyone turned to look at the table except Sutasoma who was busy devouring his sixth dosa.

"I won't," Ambika said, sternly, "And if you have a problem with that, you don't need to join our army. We don't need you."

"I already gave an *akshauhini* to the Kauravas and one to the Pandavas," the boy said, as if he was repeating it.

The other boy groaned as if *he* was sick of this, "We don't need to hear you say the same thing again and again. You can give them one and us one. It's not that hard."

"I'll be fighting against myself, though!" the first boy said, exasperated, "It'll sound like I've gone mental."

"I'm pretty sure that happened quite some time ago," Ambika muttered.

"Oh, shut it," the second boy said, annoyed, "Stop fighting over nothing."

"Seven days, Shishir," Ambika said, a note of annoyance rising into her own voice.

So, it *was* Shishir.

"Yeah, for seven days you cried. How many did you smile?" Shishir said, raising his eyebrow, "There's no point in remembering one thing if you can't remember everything."

Ambika looked at Shishir for a beat, scrutinizing him.

"You're in?" she said, once more to the first boy.

He nodded quickly.

"Fine. You better be ready tomorrow. Oh, and *you* will fight on the Pandavas' side or my brother's side. *We* need your army, not you, "Ambika said, getting up.

She walked out of the restaurant and Shishir followed. The other boy sat there for a few more seconds, which he shouldn't have done, because that was when the waiter came with the bill.

"Who was the boy?" I asked once we'd all stopped staring at the empty table.

"Which one?" Sutasoma asked.

"You didn't even see anything," I scowled.

"I heard everything," Sutasoma said.

"Not Shishir. The other one," I said.

"That's Anish," Prathivindhya said, "He's the prince of Chedi."

"Well, if Ambika doesn't want him to fight on her side, I don't want him to fight on our side," I said.

Prathivindhya shook her head, "Ambika's angry at him for something that happened a long time ago. He's a really good warrior. You want him, trust me."

I frowned but didn't say anything more.

"She seemed pretty upset," Amrita said.

"But she also seemed confident that she didn't need Anish," Satya said, "So her army must be ready too."

I looked at Satya, worried, "But she just started! How can she be done so quickly?"

"She hates her father," Prathivindhya said.

Ouch. Poor Duryodhana.

"So, what battle formation are we doing?" Sutasoma asked, his mouth full of his seventh dosa.

"Stop eating," Satya said, "And I don't know. I couldn't find any of Myna's plans. Subhadrai, why don't you choose?"

"What?" I asked, "Choose what?"

"A battle formation," Satya said.

"What formations are there to choose from?" I asked, wishing I didn't sound so stupid.

I was as bad at war research as I was with any school research. I think that instead of coming up with random stuff like toilet heaters, scientists should come up with a cure for procrastination. I'd totally buy that.

"Well, there's a lotus formation, eagle formation, crescent-moon formation, and then the famous wheel formation, *Chakravyuha*, but I wouldn't suggest that for the first day," Satya said, listing it off.

She pulled out her phone and showed me some pictures of each formation. The only one that I remembered, though, was the crescent-moon formation, so I chose that one.

She didn't seem impressed, but she didn't seem disappointed either.

"Alright. The moon, it is."

AMBIKA

FORFEIT!

"It is better to die in the path of righteousness than to live a life of sin and misery." – Arjuna, Mahabharata

Shishir and I had booked two rooms in a hotel in the kingdom of Hastinapura. It was Tuesday and we had one day for the meeting with Bhishma.

Shishir was at the Gandharva palace with the Vishakanyas and the captains of the armies we'd recruited trying to figure out our war formation.

That was something I should've been doing, but I couldn't. I wasn't going to waste my last day of a normal life holed up in the kingdom of the Gandharvas deciding whether we should make a million people look like fish or birds.

I was going to take a walk around my kingdom.

The ban on entering Hastinapura had never been applied to me, because I was never one of the original candidates for the throne, so I could roam about. It also made the fact that I'd kept the chariots in Hastinapura more believable, but I'd made King Chitrasena return *those* when I found out that they were from the devas.

Not many people were in the city, though. The huge houses were locked up and left alone until a ruler was decided for the kingdom. I took one look at the abandoned place and frantically scurried past it.

No matter how old I get, I don't think I'll ever *not* be scared of empty buildings.

Eventually, I found myself in a smaller alley than the one with the houses. It was lined with trash cans and street dogs. I passed a guy with a hood covering his face and decided that it was probably time to leave *this* street too.

I picked up my pace, but as I passed the guy he stepped forward and stopped me. I got a glance at his face when he grabbed my arm.

"You," I muttered, rolling my eyes.

Advaith.

Dussasana's son, a.k.a. Rohan's greatest minion.

"Ambika," Advaith said, exasperated, "What the hell are you doing?!"

I looked at him in confusion, "What?"

"You can't rule Hastinapura," Advaith said, "What are you thinking?!"

"Oh," I snapped, "And *Subhadrai* can rule? And *Rohan* can rule? I can rule better than the whole family put together, thank you very much."

"It's hubris to even *try!*" He said, as if he hadn't heard me, "Plus, the second you step into the throne room tomorrow for the meeting, your dad is going to strangle you to death."

"He won't get near me," I said, snobbily.

"Oh, but he has," Advaith said, clenching his fists, "Don't make me do this."

I blinked in confusion.

"What?"

He tightened his grip on my arm and pulled a knife out his pocket.

"Woah, woah," I said, quickly, "That's not fair. I'm not armed."

I ignored the knife in my pocket.

He dropped the knife and his fist crashed into my stomach, "Okay, then."

I doubled over and pulled my hand out of his tight grip, gasping for breath, "What do you want?!"

I pulled out a dagger from my pocket (Shishir had forced me to keep it and thank goodness I had). I used the hilt to punch Advaith in the mouth.

"Don't show up tomorrow," he said, picking his knife up as blood fell from his mouth, "Forfeit."

I groaned, clutching the dagger, "Nice try."

He lunged towards me, and I blocked him as he pressed his knife against mine, closer and closer towards my face.

"Whether you say yes or no, it's my job to make sure you don't show," he said, a hint of sadness in his tone.

He pressed even harder against my dagger, and I stumbled. His knife cut into my cheek, making me scream in pain.

"You still have a chance to promise me you won't show," he said.

I pressed my hand to my face and pulled it away when I realized it was wet.

Blood.

I looked up at him to see the knife plunge into my arm letting out a guttural scream as he pushed it in. He pulled it out sharply and I fell forward in excruciating pain.

I could faintly feel myself shaking in fear.

I couldn't succumb to this. I had to rule.

Why?

I groaned.

Why did I want to rule?

I bowed my head forward as I bit back the pain.

Because my father thought I couldn't. Because he thought I was worthless. Because he thought the only thing, I was good for was nothing.

But I *could* rule.

I could rule far better than Rohan and Subhadrai.

And I would prove that if it was the last thing I did. I could *not* let Advaith end it now.

Advaith knelt down, probably out of instinct, and I smacked him in the nose with my elbow.

He quickly got up, rubbing his nose and kicked me, so that my face hit the ground. The searing pain in my arm doubled as I saw the dark red blood gushing out. I squeezed my eyes and tasted the blood I'd felt on my cheek.

I tried to pick myself up, but his dark black shoe hit my head one more time pushing it onto a sharp rock on the pavement, and I succumbed to the darkness.

SUBHADRAI

THE TRIALS

"Once war has been undertaken, no peace is made by pretending there is no war." – Duryodhana, Mahabharata

I checked the clock for about the gazillionth time in the past minute. The world really was messed up. When you wanted time to pass, it wouldn't. When you didn't, it would.

Someone should really fix that. I decided to ask Satya if there was a god of time, next time she came into the room to check if I'd fallen asleep.

I waited. One minute. Twenty minutes. Thirty minutes.

I got up. That was odd. She normally came every thirty minutes.

I slowly climbed off the bed as it made a little creak sound. Amrita twitched in her sleep. I tiptoed past Sahana and swung the door open as quickly as I could, so that it wouldn't squeak.

It still did, and Amrita groaned, 'Gotosleepidiot.'

I waited for her to say more, but she didn't, so I slipped through the doorway, into the silent carpeted hallway.

I really hated walking through hotel rooms at night. It gave me the creeps, as if someone was going to jump out at me and scream-

"WHERE IS SHE?"

My head snapped towards Satya's room where the voice had come from. My heart rate seemed to have tripled as I slowly walked towards the room.

I heard a muffled voice say something and the voice came again.

"I DON'T CARE IF I WAKE UP YOUR ENTIRE HOTEL. I NEED YOU TO TELL ME WHERE SHE IS!"

I stopped outside Satya's door and hesitated. I squinted at the door and stepped back. Hopefully, some drunk dude had gotten himself stuck in the room and was blabbering something.

"I don't know where she is."

That was Satya. I stared at the door for another moment. She sounded quite calm. Maybe it wasn't anything. I was about to go back to sleep when I heard the sound of a sword being taken out of its sheath with a loud *swish*.

I swung the door open, without a moment's thought, and saw the boy I'd seen with Ambika standing in front of Satya. Except it was Satya's sword that was drawn.

"What's happening?" I asked.

"Where's Ambika?" the boy said.

I tried to recall his name, but it didn't come to my mind.

"Huh?"

"Ambika! Why are you idiots acting so dumb?!" He sounded tired, as if he'd spent all day screaming.

"Why would we know?!" I asked, equally tired (because watching almost ten movies in a row is exhausting).

He looked lost as he looked around the room, "She went missing."

I felt a tiny hope rise up to my throat, and it took everything in me not to voice it. Ambika was out of the competition! One less thing I had to worry about!

I looked at Satya to see if she felt the same thing, but she didn't look pleased, "It's not right to take out your opponents before the war, and you come and accuse a daughter of Yudhishthira of performing an act of unrighteousness?"

My mind clicked. Shishir! That was his name!

Shishir didn't seem to feel any guilt. He stared at the door as if he wished it would take him away. Being here seemed like it wouldn't help make things better.

"Why don't you go check with Rohan?!" she asked, "He would do something like kill his own sister."

Shishir glared at Satya, "She's not dead."

"Well, why don't you go find out?" Satya said, "She's not here."

"I *would* if Rohan made it as easy to find him as you made it to find you," he laughed bitterly, "Do *you* know where he is?"

Satya thought about it for a moment, "No."

"Exactly," Shishir scowled, as he brushed past me and disappeared into the darkness.

"How did he get in here?" I wondered.

"It's a hotel. Anyone can check in," Satya bit her lip, "If Rohan was willing to take his sister out of the game, he'd be more than willing to take you out too. And Ambika was actually hiding!"

I don't know what Satya was trying to convey, but when I got back into bed, it *definitely* didn't help me sleep.

***

I quickly stuffed my toothbrush into my mouth and brushed while I frantically flipped through my closet trying to find a decent outfit.

I spit out some toothpaste and muttered, "WHY DO I ONLY HAVE MY LITTLE PONY CLOTHES?!"

I heard a snicker come from the other room and glared at the door, "Amrita, do you have any normal clothes?"

"Wear a *kurti*!" Satya screamed.

I glared at the door even harder. *Kurtis* were fine, but they always made me look old.

I pulled out a dark blue *kurti* from the dark cavern of my closet and pulled it over my head. The last time I'd worn it was when I'd met the PS. When I walked out, Satya was standing in front of the door holding the keys.

"Great. You finally look Indian again," she said, with a smile, "Now let's go."

"Wait! I need to comb my hair!" I grabbed a brush from my closet as I left the room.

Satya pulled it away from me, "Nah. You don't have time. Put some oil on it and let's go."

My worst nightmares were coming true.

I rubbed some oil on my hair and stared at the mirror in disgust. Satya dragged me away from my terrible reflection and pushed me into the elevator.

"Aren't the other's coming?" I asked.

"What? You think it's a spectator sport?" Satya laughed, "This is your life at stake here, and you want an audience?!"

I quickly shook my head.

My life was at stake? What was that supposed to mean? War?

We stepped out of the elevator and into the car we'd stolen from the homeless dude. That seemed like so many eons ago… I decided that we'd return it after the war was over. I wondered how Satya had gotten it back from Mathura.

"How far away is it?" I asked, as Satya started driving.

"Two hours," Satya said, looking at me through the rear-view mirror.

I stared out the window, sighing loudly. For once in my life, that didn't feel long enough.

***

"Subhadrai."

I groaned, and I realized the car had stopped.

"Good morning, sleepyhead," Satya laughed, "Let's go. Fix your hair. You want some oil?"

"No," I said, quickly, "I'm good."

I pressed my hair against my scalp and stepped out. Rohan and a girl were standing outside his car talking with someone on the phone.

I noticed that he was wearing a shirt and jeans, and not a kurta. I shot Satya a glare and she shrugged.

The girl next to Rohan spotted me and nudged Rohan, who looked up and smirked. He whispered something to her, and she chuckled.

I tried not to stare, but I knew I'd seen the girl somewhere.

"It's Saanvi," Satya said, as if she'd read my mind, "From the boat. Remember?"

I nodded, looking around trying to spot Ambika, then remembered she was missing.

"Do you think Ambika will come?" I asked.

Satya shrugged.

I turned my attention to the huge palace before us.

So, *this* is what we were fighting for. I decided that I wouldn't mind owning it. After staring for a few minutes, I realized I only had two choices. I could own the kingdom or die.

Bhishma walked out, and frowned, "Where is your sister?"

Rohan looked up, skeptically, "How would I know?"

Bhishma stuck his head back in the kingdom and said something. He came out and gestured for us to enter.

Honestly, Bhishma was a *lot* older than I remembered. I'd never seen a person with only white hair. When I'd seen his picture in Satya's phone, he was wearing a crown, but today he looked a lot more simple and less intimidating. He also looked like he should have retired a century ago. Still, here he was. Making sure his family didn't tear each other's throats apart.

Again.

I walked towards the door with Satya following me. Rohan and Saanvi shoved past me and went in first.

"It's been so long since I've been here," Satya murmured.

I stepped into the palace, and I could feel my heart stop. There was a long golden corridor with long pillars on either side. I slowly walked down the corridor as Rohan sped past.

"Subhadrai, if you don't win the war, I'll kill you," Satya said.

I walked into the veranda which seemed to be in the middle of the palace.

There was a stone gazebo and little bushes with roses surrounding it, and a small pond in front of it. Bhishma, Duryodhana and Yudhishthira were sitting on three stone thrones waiting for us, with three ladies standing behind them expectantly.

"Welcome," Bhishma said, "Would you like some water?

I shook my head and Rohan said, "No."

Bhishma smiled, "I'm sure you're worrying about what's going to happen next. Don't worry. Come in, let's eat something. I talked to Shishir. He doesn't know if Ambika will make it or not, but let's hope she will. The choice we make depends on that."

I glanced at Rohan who bit his lip and Saanvi sighed.

Duryodhana, Yudhishthira, and Bhishma got up, and Yudhishthira shot Satya and me a smile.

Bhishma led us to a domed room with light seeping in through the wide-open door and windows. I felt my feet sink into the soft plush carpet. Behind it there were a few more doors covered in paintings of previous kings.

I blinked as light flashed on my face from the chandelier hanging from the ceiling. I felt my feet hit the wooden floor and sighed. I *loved* wooden floors. I was so sick of tiles.

There were two couches that seemed a bit more modern than I would've expected. I noticed a recliner and grinned. I *definitely* wouldn't mind living here.

Bhishma sat on one of the couches and gestured for us to sit. I sat down on the far corner of a couch and Rohan sat on the other.

A lady came in with a plate of samosas and cheeseballs.

She handed one of each to me and Rohan and set the plate on the little golden table in between the couches.

"Dig in," Bhishma said.

I glanced at Satya who was standing with Saanvi. She gestured for me to try the samosa. I did, and boy, did I regret it. It was so spicy, I could feel my face burning as I took each bite. Tears sprung to my eyes.

I glanced at Rohan who had wisely taken the cheeseball instead of the samosa.

Genius.

"So," Bhishma said, "I guess you're probably bursting with anticipation. As you know, we will have a 'test' to see who will own the throne."

He gestured to a large door with no painting, but an engraving of a large golden tree.

That was the door to the throne room. I bounced my knee up and down, and I saw Rohan wring his fingers.

"As you may have guessed," Bhishma checked the door once more and said with a sigh, "We will be hav-"

"WAIT!" came a scream from the garden.

Bhishma, Yudhishthira and Duryodhana turned to see who it was through the wide-open door beside them, and I noticed relief flood over Bhishma's face. Duryodhana turned to look at Rohan in shock.

Rohan glanced at me, then craned his neck to see who it was, but it didn't take long for us to find out.

Ambika walked through the door, her hair falling on her back in messy waves. I winced as I saw the long scars running down her face and a blood-stained cloth tied around her arm and waist.

"Wait for me."

She took a seat between Rohan and me and helped herself to a cheeseball.

In between bites, she asked, "What'd I miss?"

"Nothing," Bhishma said, "I was about to say how we'd decide the ruler."

I glanced at Rohan, who looked as if he was seeing a ghost. He probably thought he was. Saanvi looked oddly relieved too.

I looked back at Bhishma who had a large grin on his face.

"As I was saying," he continued, "We will *not* have war."

I looked at Satya who seemed as shocked as I was.

"It is time for the three of you to undertake the Trials."

GLOSSARY

Agni: The Hindu god of fire

Akshauhini: A part of an army consisting of twenty-one thousand, eight hundred seventy chariots, twenty-one thousand, eight hundred seventy elephants, sixty-five thousand six hundred ten horsemen, one hundred nine thousand, three hundred fifty-foot soldiers.

Airavata: Indra's white elephant. The king of elephants.

Amaravati: The capital of the abode of Indra. The residing area of Lord Indra.

Amma: A term used to refer to *mother*.

Anga: A kingdom in ancient India.

Apsara: A celestial being who performs in the court of Indra.

Arjuna: The third Pandava. The son of Pandu and Kunti and his celestial father was Indra. He was the most famous Pandava and a skilled archer.

Ashwatthama: A character of the original Mahabharata. He was a classmate of the Pandavas and was a close friend of Duryodhana.

Asi: A sword appearing in Hindu mythology. It is said to be the first weapon ever created. It was created to restore Dharma.

Asti: The daughter of Jarasandha and wife of Kamsa.

Asura: Celestial beings who are popularly known as the enemies of the Devas. Some Asuras can be good too.

Ayodhya: A kingdom in Ancient India. It is famous for being the home of Lord Rama.

Balarama: The elder brother of Lord Krishna. He is said to be the eighth incarnation of Lord Vishnu too.

Bhanumati: The wife of Duryodhana.

Bhima: The second Pandava. The son of Pandu and Kunti and his celestial father was Vayu. He was the strongest Pandava and was skilled in mace-fighting.

Bhishma: The supreme commander of the Kauravas. The eldest member of the family of Pandavas and Kauravas.

Brahma: A major god in Hindu mythology. Also known as 'the creator'. Part of the triumvirate consisting of him, Lord Vishnu (the preserver) and Lord Shiva (the destroyer).

Carnatic: A type of South Indian classical music.

Chedi: A kingdom in ancient India.

Chitrangada: One of the many wives of Arjuna, the princess of Manipura.

Chitrasena: A king of the Gandharvas.

Devas: Sanskrit word meaning celestial being. It is used to describe a deity in Hindu mythology.

Dharma: Path of righteousness. An important aspect of Hindu mythology.

Dhritarastra: The father of the Kauravas and the king of Hastinapura in the Mahabharata.

Dosa: A South Indian dish. A thin, savory crepe.

Drupada: The king of Panchalam and the father of Draupadi.

Duryodhana: The prince of Hastinapura and the main antagonist of the epic Mahabharata. He is the eldest Kaurava.

Dussasana: An antagonist in the Mahabharata, the brother of Duryodhana. He is the second Kaurava.

Dwaraka: A kingdom in ancient India. Famous for being the home of Lord Krishna.

Gandhari: The mother of Duryodhana, Dussasana and other Kauravas. The wife of Dhritarastra and the sister of Shakuni.

Gandharva: A celestial being known for their musical qualities.

Gandiva: The legendary bow of Arjuna.

Ganga: A holy river flowing through India. Also appears in the form of a goddess. The mother of Bhishma and the wife of Shantanu.

Hanuman: An important figure in the Ramayana. A deity in Hindu mythology, and a devoted companion of Lord Rama. Appears in the form of part man, part monkey.

Indra: The king of devas and heaven in Hindu mythology, and the god of the sky. He is the celestial father of Arjuna.

Indraprastha: A kingdom in ancient India. Famous for being the kingdom of the Pandavas.

Jarasandha: The king of the kingdom of Magadha. One of the most powerful rulers in Hindu mythology.

Kalinga Narthana Thillana: A Carnatic song composed by *Oothakkada Venkata Kavi*.

Kamsa: The king of the kingdom of Mathura. The main antagonist in the story of Krishna.

Kheer: An Indian sweet/pudding.

Krishna: A major Hindu god. He is the ninth incarnation of Lord Vishnu and the cousin of the Pandavas in the Mahabharata.

Kubera: The god of wealth and ruler of the Gandharvas.

Kunti: The mother of Yudhishthira, Bhima, and Arjuna. She raised the Pandavas and is one of the panchakanyas.

Kurti: A traditional garment worn in India.

Kurukshetra War: The legendary war described in the Mahabharata between the Pandavas and Kauravas.

Laddu: A spherical delicacy. It is the most ancient Indian sweet.

Lakshman: The son of Duryodhana and Bhanumati.

Lakshmana: The brother of Lord Rama and a prince of the kingdom of Ayodhya.

Lakshmanaa: The daughter of Duryodhana and Bhanumati.

Lakshmi: The wife of Lord Vishnu and the goddess of wealth and prosperity.

Madra: A kingdom in ancient India.

Madri: The princess of Madra. She is the wife of Pandu and the mother of Nakula and Sahadeva.

Magadha: A kingdom in ancient India.

Mahabharata: One of the two most important Sanskrit epics in Hindu mythology. It is the longest poem ever written and was narrated by Sage Veda Vyasa. It describes the struggle for the throne of Hastinapura.

Malayadhwaja: A king in ancient Southern India who helped the Pandavas in their war.

Marut: Maruts are celestial beings. They are violent and powerful storm deities.

Mathura: A kingdom in ancient India. It is famous for being the birthplace of Lord Krishna.

Nagas: A race of half-serpent and half-human beings.

Nakula: The fourth Pandava. The son of Pandu and Madri and his celestial father were one of the Ashwini Twins. He was the most handsome Pandava and was a skilled swordsman.

Panchakanyas: A group of the five most iconic, powerful, and beautiful women in Hindu Mythology. They are *Ahalya, Tara, Mandodari, Draupadi* and *Kunti*.

THE SWORDS CLASH

Panchalam: A kingdom in ancient India. Famous for being the home of Draupadi.

Pandavas: The five sons of Pandu and the heroes of the Mahabharata. They are Yudhishthira, Bhima, Arjuna, Nakula and Sahadeva.

Pandu: The brother of Dhritarastra, the father of the Pandavas, and the husband of Kunti and Madri.

Prapti: The daughter of Jarasandha and the wife of Kamsa.

Prathivindhya: The son of Yudhishthira and Draupadi.

Rakshasa: A powerful mythological being. Depicted as demons and evil spirits.

Rama: A major Hindu deity. The main character of the epic Ramayana and the seventh incarnation of Lord Vishnu.

Ramayana: One of the two most important Sanskrit epics in Hindu mythology. It was written down by Sage Valmiki. It describes the journey of the seventh incarnation of Lord Vishnu, Rama.

Rishi: An enlightened person or sage.

Rukmi: The brother of Rukmini and good friend of Shishupala. He was the ruler of the kingdom Vidarbha.

Rukmini: The princess of Vidarbha. She is said to be an incarnation of the Goddess Lakshmi and the wife of Krishna.

Sahadeva: The youngest Pandava and child of Madri. He was a skilled astrologist and swordsman.

Sanskrit: An ancient classical language. Probably the second oldest language still in use today. Most ancient Hindu scriptures are written in this language.

Sari: A traditional garment worn by women in India.

Satanika: The son of Nakula and Draupadi.

Satyavati: The wife of Shantanu and the great-grandmother of the Pandavas and Kauravas.

Shakuni: The ruler of the kingdom of Gandharva and the brother of Gandhari. He corrupted Duryodhana and is hence the main reason for the Kurukshetra war.

Shantanu: The father of Bhishma and the great-grandfather of the Pandavas and Kauravas. He is the husband of Satyavati and Ganga.

Shatrughna: One of the princes of Ayodhya and the brother of Lord Rama.

Shishupala: A close friend of Duryodhana, and a cousin of Lord Krishna and the Pandavas. He is the ruler of the kingdom of Chedi.

Shrutakarma: The son of Arjuna and Draupadi.

Shrutasena: The son of Sahadeva and Draupadi.

Sindhu: A kingdom in ancient India. It is famous for being the kingdom of Jarasandha, the brother-in-law of Duryodhana.

Sita: The princess of the kingdom of Mithila. She is said to be an incarnation of Goddess Lakshmi and the wife of Lord Rama.

Subhadra: She is said to be an incarnation of the Goddess *Durga* and the sister of Krishna. She was one of the wives of Arjuna and the mother of Abhimanyu.

Surya: The Hindu god of the sun.

Sutasoma: The son of Bhima and Draupadi.

Syamantaka Gem: Also known as the Sun jewel, it is a jewel created by Surya. It is a divine gem in Hindu mythology with powerful abilities.

Takshaka: A naga king who used to live in the forest of Indraprastha before Arjuna burnt down half of the forest killing most of his family.

Ulupi: A *Nagini* princess with a jewel that can bring a person back from death. She is one of Arjuna's wives.

Upapandavas: The sons of the Pandavas and Draupadi. It means "junior Pandavas".

Uttarai: The princess of the kingdom of Matsya. She was the wife of Abhimanyu in the Mahabharata and the mother of the last surviving descendant of the Pandavas, Parikshit.

Vasudeva: The father of Lord Krishna. He was a Yadava prince and the brother of Kunti.

Vayu: The Hindu god of wind. He is the celestial father of Bhima.

Vishakanyas: Female assassins who were fed poisoned and trained to kill.

Vyuha: A war formation. An arrangement for battle troops.

Yadu: A king in Hindu Mythology. His descendants are known as Yadavas, and he founded the Yadu dynasty.

Yaksha: A celestial being. They are nature spirits and are under the rule of Kubera.

Yama: The god of Death and Righteousness. He is also known as Dharma Raja. He is the celestial father of Yudhishthira.

ACKNOWLEDGEMENTS

When a fourteen-year-old writes a book, she's going to ask someone for help. I was no exception. I think that this section of the book has more drafts than any other, because it's *so* important that I don't miss anybody. Needless to say, there is *no* way I could have ever done this myself.

Amma and Appa, thank you for supporting me the whole way through and for not laughing your heads off when your eleven-year-old daughter told you that she'd written a book. Thank you even more for *letting* your fifteen-year-old publish a book. I doubt I would have ever started writing if you hadn't made me enjoy reading as much as I do today. Not to mention, you told me the Mahabharata! I can't imagine a life without those stories that you kept safe for me to know one day.

Next, I'd like to thank my sister, Vasundhara, who's read every draft of the book (which were probably traumatic experiences. I've written some stupid stuff). If it weren't for you constantly devouring my book, I wouldn't have gone past the first chapter. It's been a long three-year journey, but you stayed by Subhadrai for every page.

Also, I would like to thank Neela for trying (*cough* trying *cough*) her best not to bother me while I was writing.

A huge, huge, huge thanks to my editor, Elizabeth Stranahan for making it such an *amazing* experience to work with her. I've never looked forward to corrections more than I did yours. You turned my dry, messy, childish first draft into a beautiful masterpiece. You're the *best*, Liz!

Shishir! I named a character after you, just like you asked, although you aren't the megalomaniac villain you hoped to be. And Girish Periappa, look, I *finally* published!

Sannu, I hope you're happy with the little favor I've done you, and Ashray, all those cricket references are all dedicated to you 😊.

A huge thanks to the rest of my family who inspired more of this story than they'll ever know.

I'd also like to thank Veda Vyasa, the author of the original Mahabharata for having written down a masterpiece like that. Wherever you are, you're the best.

I'd also like to acknowledge that kid in sixth grade who proudly told me that the Pandavas were Rama, Lakshmana, and Sita.

Look what you made me do.

And to my friends who reminded me not to get lost in my story and once in a while dragged me off to P.E., It takes a lot of strength to do that, and I appreciate it. You know who you are, and you deserve a trophy, guys.

Speaking of P.E., I would also like to acknowledge all those P.E.s I missed because of the book (Not like I would've gone either ways).

Most importantly, though, thank *you* for sticking with Subhadrai for this long. Don't worry, there's more coming, but until then, I can't begin to express my gratitude towards you. *You* made this story possible, <3.